Betty's Best

SIMPLE COMFORT FOOD FROM GRANDMA'S KITCHEN

BETTY ROHDE

Gibbs Smith, Publisher
TO ENRICH AND INSPIRE HUMANKIND
Salt Lake City | Charleston | Santa Fe | Santa Barbara

First Edition
12 11 10 09 08   5 4 3 2 1

Text © 2008 Betty Rohde

All rights reserved. No part of this book may be reproduced by any means whatsoever without written permission from the publisher, except brief portions quoted for purpose of review.

Published by
Gibbs Smith, Publisher
P.O. Box 667
Layton, Utah 84041

Orders: 1.800.835.4993
www.gibbs-smith.com

Designed by Mary Ellen Thompson
Printed and bound in Canada

Library of Congress Cataloging-in-Publication Data

Rohde, Betty.
  Betty's best : simple comfort food from grandma's kitchen / Betty Rohde.
 — 1st ed.
     p. cm.
  ISBN-13: 978-1-4236-0244-6
  ISBN-10: 1-4236-0244-7
  1. Cookery, American. 2. Comfort food. I. Title.

TX715.R72775 2008
641.5973—dc22

2007041423

Contents

5 Introduction
7 Cakes and Frostings
27 Pies and Crusts
45 Cookies
57 Breads
73 Breakfast
83 Salads
95 Side Dishes
111 Poultry
123 Meats
131 Metric Conversion Chart
132 Index

To Bob, my love . . .

Who now lives with Grandma.
He married a young thing, thin and feisty.
My hair didn't fall out like yours,
But it has gotten a lot lighter.
I think bald is beautiful, especially on you.
But after all, if you have to live with a grandma
That means I get to live with a grandpa.
Every day is a new day to us; we don't do the same thing twice.
We do thank God every day for what we have and thank him
    for our children and
Grandchildren, ask him to be with our country,
I think that just about says it all.
We will still be here together, cooking, testing, praying and playing
Next book around. Hope it is a piece of "cake."
"I Do" "I Did" "I Will" till death do us part.
                                      Amen. Me

I would like to acknowledge my grandmothers with an extra
    little dedication for this book to them.

Thanks Ma and Daddaw!

Thank you, Bob, for all your help and support.
Eternal love surrounds you.

Introduction

I have many memories of days spent with my grandmas in their kitchens learning about life. A big portion of their lives were spent in the kitchen. They taught me to cook, to listen, to love, to care, to feel, to gossip, to share, to shut up and to work.

I can still see my grandmothers making their special dishes. Neither cooked the same, nor can I ever remember eating the same thing at the other grandmother's house.

The specialty of my maternal grandmother, Daddaw, was canning and preserving. My grandfather, Pappa, used to say, "she canned everything but the dish rag, and sometimes that was questionable."

Daddaw was a soft-spoken, God-fearing lamb of a lady. She never played games with me; she was always too busy with her day-to-day chores. That is where I came in. I followed her around and tried to help. All the time I was just getting a few lessons on life. She never told me I was too little to try anything. Whatever it was, she let me try, and most of the time I did a pretty good job. When I was a kid, about five or six years old, I had to do and know things that a twelve- to fourteen-year-old does and knows today. I had to grow up faster as it was a necessity of life to help, especially on the farm.

My paternal grandmother, Ma, on the other hand, was the total opposite of Daddaw. She was a firm, stern, matronly, hair in bun, bible thumping sort of person. I was taught things that are priceless, the old-fashioned way, like how to make potato salad, chicken and dumplings, turkey and dressing, pumpkin pie—all the great holiday specials. Ma made them and was a wonderful cook. Her specialty was cooking everything—the old-fashioned way and good.

I wonder sometimes when I am making a holiday dinner how they did it. I have two kitchens with three ranges, three ovens, plus an electric roaster that I bake the turkey or ham in. I stuff things into three refrigerators, wondering how in the world and where in the world they put it all.

They had such routines, the same every time. You knew what would be on the table when you went to Ma's or Daddaw's for holidays. Sunday dinners were just about the same: chicken out of the yard, vegetables out of the garden or canned goods. It isn't any different today at our house—if I don't have each grand's favorite dish, I am in trouble.

The recipes in this book were my grandmothers' old recipes—they taught me.

Cakes & Frostings

CAKES & FROSTINGS

TIPS & HINTS FOR CAKES & FROSTINGS

- Butter or margarine, eggs and milk all should be at room temperature for best results. Take them out of the refrigerator about 2 hours before using.

- Don't cut your time short when creaming. It takes time to incorporate air for a light texture. Allow more than 10 minutes if using a portable mixer. Insufficiently creaming cake batter will result in a coarse texture. A heavy, compact texture is a result of extreme overbeating.

- Skip sifting. Remember when every recipe said "sift"? Just stir the flour in the canister, lightly spoon it into the measuring cup and level off with a straight-edged knife or metal spatula. Take care not to tap or shake the measuring cup as you fill it. Correct measurements are very important in successful baking.

- Thorough mixing is a must! When adding dry ingredients and milk, beat just until blended after each addition, scraping the sides and the bottom of the bowl constantly. Then beat a few seconds longer.

- Spread the batter evenly to the sides of the pan. Tap pans lightly on the counter to remove large air bubbles.

- Place pans near the center of the oven. Don't let pans touch each other or the sides of the oven. Don't place pans directly under each other; stagger them on two shelves.

CAKES & FROSTINGS

- To keep your cakes from having a floury look, dust the pans with cocoa powder mixed with powdered sugar after greasing and flouring.

- Adding two tablespoons oil to cake mixes keeps them moist and less crumbly.

- Use a cake tester, or toothpick, to check if the cake is done. Stick it in the center of the cake—if no batter comes out on the tester, the cake is done. The old-fashioned way was to lightly touch the center of the cake—if it bounced back it was done. If it kept fingerprints it wasn't done.

- To help make your powdered sugar icings stay moist and not crack, add a pinch of baking powder.

- First frost with a very thin layer and set aside for a short time. Then evenly apply a second coat.

- To keep your icings from becoming grainy, add a pinch of salt to your sugar.

- To keep frosting from soaking through the cake, sprinkle the top of each cake layer with powdered sugar, and then frost.

CAKES & FROSTINGS

Carrot Cake

- 3 cups flour
- 2 cups sugar
- 2 teaspoons cinnamon
- 2 teaspoons baking soda
- 1/2 teaspoon salt
- 2 cups grated carrots
- 1-1/2 cups canola oil
- 1 (8-ounce) can crushed pineapple, lightly drained
- 1-1/2 cups nuts, chopped
- 3 eggs

• • • • • • • • • • • •

Mix dry ingredients and blend well. Stir in carrots, oil, pineapple and nuts. Add eggs one at a time, stirring after each addition. Bake in a greased and floured Bundt pan at 350 degrees F for 60 minutes, or until done.

Makes 12 servings

CAKES & FROSTINGS

Banana Nut Cake

1-1/2 cups sugar
1/2 cup butter
2 eggs
3 bananas, divided
1 teaspoon baking soda

4 tablespoons buttermilk
1-1/2 cups flour
1 cup nuts, chopped
1 teaspoon vanilla

• • • • • • • • • •

Cream sugar and butter; add well-beaten eggs. Mash bananas fine, and then add half of them to the mixture. Stir baking soda into buttermilk, and then add to the mixture. Add remaining bananas, flour, nuts and vanilla. Bake in two well-greased 9-inch round pans at 350 degrees F for 30 to 40 minutes, or until toothpick inserted in center comes out clean. Cool on wire rack, and then frost with favorite frosting. This cake may also be baked in a loaf pan.

Makes 12 servings

CAKES & FROSTINGS

Banana Split Cake

- 1-1/2 cups margarine, divided
- 2 cups graham cracker crumbs
- 1 cup powdered sugar
- 2 eggs
- 4 bananas, thinly sliced
- 2 cups crushed pineapple, drained
- 1 (8-ounce) container frozen whipped topping, thawed
- 1 cup nuts, chopped
- Maraschino cherries, optional

• • • • • • • • • • • •

Melt 1/2 cup margarine and then combine with graham cracker crumbs. Firmly press in bottom of a 9 x 13-inch pan; set aside. Combine remaining margarine, powdered sugar and eggs with a hand mixer. Mix until fluffy, about 15 minutes. Spread mixture over graham cracker crumbs. Place sliced bananas over mixture, spread pineapple over bananas and spread whipped topping over pineapple. Top with nuts and maraschino cherries, and then refrigerate overnight. Cut into squares before serving.

Note: Plan ahead for this cake as it needs to refrigerate overnight. Ultra pasteurized eggs should be used since the cake is not baked.

MAKES 12 SERVINGS

CAKES & FROSTINGS

Brownie Sheet Cake

1 cup water
1 cup margarine
1/4 cup cocoa
2 cups sugar
2 cups flour

1 teaspoon baking soda
1 to 2 teaspoons cinnamon
2 eggs
1/2 cup buttermilk

Frosting
1/3 cup buttermilk
1/2 cup margarine
1/4 cup cocoa
1 (16-ounce) box powdered sugar
1 cup pecans, chopped

Put water, margarine and cocoa in a saucepan and heat to a boil. In a bowl blend sugar, flour, baking soda and cinnamon; stir into cocoa mixture. Add eggs and buttermilk and beat well. Pour into a greased 15 x 10 x 1-inch jellyroll pan. Bake at 400 degrees F for 20 minutes. Spread with frosting while still hot.

Frosting
Bring buttermilk and margarine to just boiling. Pour over cocoa blended with powdered sugar and beat until creamy; stir in pecans.

Makes 15 servings

CAKES & FROSTINGS

Crushed Pineapple Cake

- 2 cups flour
- 2 teaspoons baking soda
- 1/2 teaspoon salt
- 1-1/2 cups sugar
- 2 eggs
- 1/4 cup vegetable oil
- 2 cups crushed pineapple, with liquid
- 1/2 cup firmly packed brown sugar
- 1/2 cup nuts, chopped
- 1/2 cup coconut

Icing
- 3/4 cup sugar
- 1/2 cup evaporated milk
- 1/2 cup margarine

Combine flour, baking soda and salt; set aside. Beat sugar and eggs together, and then add oil. Mix in flour mixture. Stir in pineapple. Pour batter into a greased and floured 9 x 13-inch pan. Sprinkle brown sugar mixed with nuts and coconut over top. Bake at 325 degrees F for 45 to 60 minutes, or until done.

Icing
While cake is baking, combine sugar, evaporated milk and margarine in a heavy saucepan. Bring to a boil for 1 minute. Poke holes in the cake with a fork, and then pour icing over hot cake.

MAKES 12 SERVINGS

CAKES & FROSTINGS

Fruit Cocktail Cake

2 cups flour
1-1/2 cups sugar
2 teaspoons baking soda
2 eggs, beaten
1 (15-ounce) can fruit cocktail, with liquid

Icing
1/2 cup margarine
1 cup sugar
1/2 cup evaporated milk
1/2 cup pecans, chopped
1 cup coconut

• • • • • • • • • • •

Mix flour, sugar and baking soda together. Add eggs and fruit cocktail, and then mix with a hand mixer. Pour into a greased and floured 9 x 13-inch baking pan. Bake at 350 degrees F for about 40 to 45 minutes. Check often for doneness.

Icing
Combine margarine, sugar and evaporated milk in a saucepan, and then bring to a boil for 2 minutes. Add pecans and coconut, and then pour over cake while hot.

Note: This cake may also be baked in a loaf pan for 1 hour at 325 degrees F.

MAKES 12 SERVINGS

CAKES & FROSTINGS

Johnny Cake

1 cup flour
1 cup yellow cornmeal
1 teaspoon baking soda
1/2 teaspoon salt
2 tablespoons sugar

1 egg, well beaten
3/4 cup milk
1/4 cup vinegar
1/4 cup shortening, melted

• • • • • • • • • • • •

Combine flour, cornmeal, baking soda, salt and sugar. In a separate bowl, mix egg, milk and vinegar together. Mix milk mixture into the dry mixture, and then add shortening; stir only until dry ingredients are moistened. Pour into a greased 8 x 8-inch baking pan. Bake at 400 degrees F for 30 to 35 minutes, or until done.

Makes 8 servings

CAKES & FROSTINGS

One Egg Cake

3 tablespoons shortening
1 cup sugar
1 egg, beaten
1 cup milk

2 cups flour
1/4 teaspoon salt
2 teaspoons baking powder
1 teaspoon vanilla

• • • • • • • • • • • •

Cream shortening, and then add sugar and egg. Alternately add milk and flour mixed with salt and baking powder; add vanilla. Bake in one 8-inch cake pan at 350 degrees F for about 25 minutes. Use any frosting.

MAKES 4 TO 6 SERVINGS

CAKES & FROSTINGS

Lemon Gelatin Cake

- 1 (3-ounce) box lemon gelatin
- 1 cup boiling water
- 1 yellow cake mix
- 3/4 cup canola oil
- 4 eggs
- 1 teaspoon lemon juice
- 1 teaspoon lemon rind

Icing
- 1-1/3 cups powdered sugar
- 4 tablespoons lemon juice

• • • • • • • • • • •

Dissolve gelatin in water, and then cool to room temperature. Mix cake mix and oil together, and then add eggs one at a time; beat until smooth. Add cooled gelatin mixture, and then lemon juice and rind. Bake in a greased loaf pan for 40 minutes at 350 degrees F.

Icing
Mix powdered sugar and lemon juice together, and then spread on cake while hot.

MAKES 8 SERVINGS

CAKES & FROSTINGS

Mississippi Mud Cake

1 cup margarine
2 cups sugar
1/2 cup cocoa
4 eggs
1-1/2 cups flour
1/2 cup nuts, chopped
1-1/3 cups coconut
1 (7-ounce) jar marshmallow creme

Icing
1/2 cup margarine, melted
1/3 cup cocoa
1 (16-ounce) box powdered sugar
5 tablespoons evaporated milk
1 teaspoon vanilla
1/2 cup nuts, chopped

• • • • • • • • • • •

Cream together margarine, sugar and cocoa. Add eggs one at a time, beating after each addition. Add flour and mix well, and then add nuts and coconut. Pour into a 15 x 10 x 1-inch greased and floured jellyroll pan. Bake at 350 degrees F for 40 minutes. Spread marshmallow creme over hot cake.

Icing

Stir margarine and cocoa together, and then cook in a saucepan for about 1 minute. Add powdered sugar, evaporated milk, vanilla and nuts. Mix well, and then spread over marshmallow layer.

Makes 15 servings

CAKES & FROSTINGS

Oatmeal Cake

- 1 cup quick-cooking oats
- 1-1/2 cups boiling water
- 1 cup firmly packed brown sugar
- 1 cup sugar
- 2 eggs
- 1/2 cup butter, softened
- 1-1/2 cups flour
- 1 teaspoon baking soda
- 1 teaspoon cinnamon
- Pinch of salt
- 1 teaspoon vanilla
- 1 teaspoon burnt sugar flavoring*

Topping
- 1/2 cup coconut
- 1 cup firmly packed brown sugar
- 1/4 cup cream
- 1 teaspoon vanilla
- 1/2 cup pecans, chopped

• • • • • • • • • • •

Stir oats into boiling water; let stand while combining other ingredients. Combine sugars, eggs, butter, flour, baking soda, cinnamon and salt, in order given, with a hand mixer. Add oatmeal mixture, vanilla and burnt sugar flavoring. Bake in a greased and floured 9 x 13-inch baking pan at 350 degrees F for about 40 to 45 minutes.

Topping

Combine all topping ingredients, and then spread on warm cake. Place under broiler until lightly browned and bubbly—watch closely.

Note: This cake is very moist and freezes well.

*If not available use maple flavoring.

MAKES 12 SERVINGS

CAKES & FROSTINGS

Pumpkin Cake

- 1/2 cup shortening
- 1 cup sugar
- 1 cup firmly packed brown sugar
- 2 eggs, beaten
- 1 cup cooked and mashed, or canned pumpkin (may use squash instead)
- 3 cups cake flour
- 4 teaspoons baking powder
- 1/4 teaspoon baking soda
- 1/2 cup milk
- 1 cup walnuts, chopped
- 1 teaspoon maple extract

• • • • • • • • • •

Cream shortening, and then add sugars, eggs and pumpkin. Combine flour, baking powder and baking soda; add alternately with milk to pumpkin mixture. Fold in walnuts and maple extract. Pour into three greased 8-inch cake pans. Bake at 350 degrees F for 30 minutes, or until done. Cool and frost with Harvest Moon Frosting (see recipe on page 26).

Makes 12 servings

CAKES & FROSTINGS

Nola's Pineapple Cake

- 1 yellow (butter) cake mix
- 1 (20-ounce) can crushed pineapple, with liquid
- 1 (8-ounce) package cream cheese, softened
- 1 (1.5-ounce) box vanilla instant pudding, made according to directions
- 1 (12-ounce) container frozen whipped topping, thawed
- 1-1/2 cups coconut
- Maraschino cherries for garnish

• • • • • • • • • • • •

Bake cake mix in a 9 x 13-inch pan according to directions; cool slightly. Punch holes in cake with a fork, and then top with pineapple. Beat cream cheese until smooth, and then add to prepared pudding. Spread over pineapple. Mix whipped topping with coconut, and then spread over pudding mixture. Add cherries if desired. Cut into squares to serve.

MAKES 12 SERVINGS

CAKES & FROSTINGS

Strawberry Cake

- 1 white cake mix
- 1 (3-ounce) box strawberry gelatin
- 3 tablespoons flour
- 4 eggs
- 1 cup canola oil
- 1/2 cup water
- Pinch of salt
- 1 cup frozen strawberries, thawed and drained, juice reserved
- 1 cup pecans, chopped

Glaze
- 1/2 (16-ounce) box powdered sugar
- 1/2 cup margarine, softened
- 1/2 cup reserved strawberry juice

• • • • • • • • • • •

Mix cake mix, gelatin mix and flour together. Add eggs, oil, water and salt. Mix well with a hand mixer, and then add strawberries and pecans. Bake in two well greased and floured 9-inch cake pans or a 9 x 13-inch cake pan at 350 degrees F for 30 to 40 minutes.

Glaze
Mix sugar, margarine and juice together. Pour over cake when about half cool.

Makes 12 servings

CAKES & FROSTINGS

Cocoa Frosting

1 cup powdered sugar
Pinch of salt
2 tablespoons cocoa

2 tablespoons butter, melted
3 tablespoons hot coffee
1/2 teaspoon vanilla

• • • • • • • • • • •

Blend sugar, salt, cocoa and butter together using a hand mixer. Add enough hot coffee to make smooth mixture; add vanilla.

Makes enough to frost one 9-inch layer cake

Brown Sugar Frosting

3 cups firmly packed brown sugar
1/4 cup butter

1-1/2 cups cream
1 teaspoon vanilla

• • • • • • • • • • •

Mix the first three ingredients together thoroughly. Cook mixture to soft-ball stage using a candy thermometer. Remove from heat, beat until creamy, and then add vanilla.

Makes enough to frost one 9 x 13-inch cake or tops of two cake layers

CAKES & FROSTINGS

Seven-Minute Frosting

2 egg whites
Pinch of salt
1-1/2 cups sugar
1 tablespoon white corn syrup

4 tablespoons cold water
1/4 teaspoon cream of tartar
1 teaspoon vanilla

• • • • • • • • • • • •

Beat everything except vanilla in the top of a double boiler. Use a hand mixer to beat while double boiler is over boiling water; beat briskly until mixture will stand in peaks, about 7 minutes. Remove from water, cool a few minutes, add vanilla and beat until cold. If too stiff, add hot water by teaspoon, one at time, beating briskly.

MAKES ENOUGH TO FROST ONE 9-INCH LAYER CAKE OR 2 DOZEN CUPCAKES

Variations

Brown Sugar Sea Foam
Substitute 2 cups firmly packed light brown sugar for the white sugar.

Chocolate Frosting
Beat in 3/4 cup cocoa blended with 3 to 4 tablespoons hot water just before spreading on cake.

Caramel Frosting
Use 1 cup firmly packed brown sugar in place of white sugar; flavor with 1/2 teaspoon maple flavoring.

CAKES & FROSTINGS

Basic Glaze

1 cup powdered sugar
1 tablespoon milk

1/2 teaspoon vanilla

• • • • • • • • • • •

Mix sugar with milk and vanilla using a wire whisk until smooth. Drizzle over cakes or cookies.

Makes 1/2 to 3/4 cup glaze

Harvest Moon Frosting

3 egg whites, unbeaten
1-1/2 cups firmly packed
   brown sugar

Dash of salt
6 tablespoons water
1 teaspoon vanilla

• • • • • • • • • • •

Combine all ingredients except vanilla in a double boiler; beat well using a hand mixer. Place over rapidly boiling water and cook 7 minutes, beating constantly, or until frosting stands in peaks. Remove from boiling water; then add vanilla and stir. Beat until thick enough to spread.

Makes enough to frost one 9 x 13-inch cake or one 9-inch layer cake

Pies & Crusts

PIES & CRUSTS

TIPS & HINTS FOR PIES & CRUSTS

- Keep the juices from soaking into the pie crust when making a fruit pie by brushing the bottom crust with egg whites.

- Add a teaspoon of vinegar to pie dough for a flaky crust.

- Warm the pie pan before adding the bottom pie crust to keep it from becoming soggy or soft.

- For an extra-flaky crust, use ice-cold sour cream or whipping cream instead of water. If using water or milk, be sure that it is ice cold.

- Chill your pie dough before rolling it so the crust will hold its shape better and not shrink as much.

- When making a cream-filled pie, coat the crust with sugar before adding the filling to prevent the crust from being soggy.

- Check the center of a pie with a sharp knife to test for doneness—when the knife comes out clean, the pie is done.

PIES & CRUSTS

- Add a pinch of baking powder to room temperature egg whites before beating them for meringue. As you are gradually beating the eggs, add 2 to 3 tablespoons sugar for each egg white. Perfect peaks should stand up tall and not fall over.

- To perk up meringue peaks, add 1/4 teaspoon white vinegar for each 3 egg whites while beating.

- To keep meringues from weeping, turn off the oven before the meringue finishes cooking and leave it in the oven until it cools down.

> *Do you remember...*
> *the ration stamps you had to have to get chocolate during WWII? Dates me, doesn't it! I remember going over to my grandmother's house on Sunday, and she would have one of these chocolate pies sitting up on the top of the old wood cooking stove, cooling. I just couldn't wait until the end of dinner so I could have a taste of that chocolate—oh, so good. Times gone forever, but I still have the pie recipe to share.*

PIES & CRUSTS

Chocolate Pie

1 cup sugar
4 tablespoons flour
3 tablespoons cocoa
Pinch of salt
2 cups milk
3 eggs, separated
2 tablespoons butter
1 (9-inch) baked pie crust

Meringue
2 egg whites, room temperature
3 tablespoons sugar
1/2 teaspoon lemon juice
1/4 teaspoon vanilla

• • • • • • • • • • • •

Mix sugar, flour, cocoa and salt together in a heavy saucepan. Stir in milk and egg yolks. Cook over medium heat until thick. Remove from heat and add butter. Let cool 5 minutes, and then pour into baked crust.

For meringue, beat egg whites until frothy; start slowly, adding sugar a little at a time until all is added. Beating on high, add lemon juice and vanilla and continue beating until it is stiff and forming peaks. Top pie with meringue, sealing around edges and bake at 350 degrees F for 15 to 25 minutes, until lightly brown. Watch closely. For thick meringues, bake at 300 to 325 degrees F for 20 to 30 minutes, depending on thickness.

Makes 8 servings

PIES & CRUSTS

Apple Pie

3/4 to 1 cup sugar, reserving 2 tablespoons to sprinkle on crust
1 teaspoon cinnamon or nutmeg

6 to 7 apples, peeled and thinly sliced
2 (9-inch) pie crusts
1-1/2 tablespoons butter

• • • • • • • • • • •

Mix sugar and cinnamon or nutmeg. Toss apple slices in sugar mixture. Place apples in bottom pie crust, dot with butter and cover with remaining crust. Sprinkle sugar lightly over top of crust. Poke top crust with a fork or knife to vent. Bake at 400 degrees F for 40 to 50 minutes, or until the apples are tender. Check with sharp knife, but be careful not to punch a hole in bottom crust.

Makes 8 servings

PIES & CRUSTS

Coconut Custard Pie

- 1 (9-inch) pie crust
- 1 cup sugar
- 1 tablespoon flour
- 3 large eggs, lightly beaten
- 1 (3.5-ounce) can sweetened coconut
- 1/2 cup evaporated milk
- 1/3 cup butter or margarine, melted
- 1 teaspoon vanilla

• • • • • • • • • • •

Bake pie crust for 10 minutes at 400 degrees F; remove, set aside and reduce oven temperature to 325 degrees F. Combine sugar and flour, and then add eggs. Add coconut, evaporated milk, butter and vanilla. Pour filling into baked crust. Bake for 35 to 40 minutes, or until set. Check with knife in center to see if it is set.

MAKES 6 SERVINGS

PIES & CRUSTS

Ruby's Custard Pie

3 eggs
5 tablespoons sugar
1/8 teaspoon salt
1/4 teaspoon nutmeg

1/2 teaspoon vanilla
2 cups scalded milk
1 (9-inch) unbaked pie crust

• • • • • • • • • • •

Beat eggs until yolks and whites are blended. Add sugar, salt, nutmeg and vanilla; mix thoroughly. Add milk slowly, stirring constantly. Pour into pie crust. Bake at 425 degrees F for 15 minutes, and then reduce heat to 350 degrees F and bake an additional 25 to 35 minutes, or until done to the knife test.

Makes 8 servings

PIES & CRUSTS

Five-Layer Pie

- 1 cup flour
- 1/2 cup margarine, room temperature
- Dash of salt
- 1/2 cup nuts, chopped
- 1 (8-ounce) package cream cheese, softened
- 1 cup powdered sugar
- 1 (16-ounce) container frozen whipped topping, thawed and divided
- 1 (3-ounce) box any flavor instant pudding, mixed according to directions

• • • • • • • • • • •

Mix flour, margarine, salt and nuts, and then press firmly into the bottom of a 9 x 13-inch pan. Bake at 350 degrees F for 15 to 20 minutes; let cool. Mix cream cheese, powdered sugar and 2/3 cup whipped topping; spread over crust. Spread pudding over cream cheese layer, and then cover with remaining whipped topping. Garnish with nuts or chocolate shavings, and then refrigerate until ready to serve.

Makes 12 servings

PIES & CRUSTS

Millionaire Pie

Crust
3 egg whites
1 cup sugar
1/2 teaspoon salt
1/2 teaspoon vanilla
21 Ritz crackers, crushed

Filling
1 (8-ounce) package cream cheese, softened
3 tablespoons milk
3/4 cup powdered sugar

Top Layer
1 (8-ounce) can crushed pineapple, drained
1/2 cup pecans, chopped
1-1/2 cups whipped cream

• • • • • • • • • • • •

Crust
Beat egg whites until stiff. Add sugar, salt and vanilla, and mix together; fold in crackers. Press into a 9-inch pie plate. Bake at 350 degrees F for 25 minutes. Completely cool crust.

Filling
Mix cream cheese, milk and powdered sugar together using a hand mixer. Line crust with this mixture.

Top Layer
Spread the drained pineapple over the cream cheese layer, sprinkle pecans over pineapple, and then cover with whipped cream. Refrigerate for at least 2 to 3 hours before serving.

Makes 8 servings

PIES & CRUSTS

Frozen Fluffy Strawberry Pie

- 1/3 cup butter or margarine
- 2-1/2 cups coconut, lightly toasted
- 1 (3-ounce) package cream cheese, softened
- 1 (14-ounce) can sweetened condensed milk
- 2-1/2 cups mashed fresh or frozen strawberries, unsweetened
- 3 tablespoons lemon juice
- 1 cup whipped cream

• • • • • • • • • • •

Melt butter, and then mix well with coconut. Press into bottom of a 9-inch pie plate, and then chill. Beat cream cheese until fluffy, and then add condensed milk. Stir in strawberries and lemon juice; fold in whipped cream. Pour mixture into the coconut crust, and then freeze 4 hours, or until firm.

Makes 8 servings

PIES & CRUSTS

Fresh Strawberry Pie

- 1 cup sugar
- 3 tablespoons cornstarch
- 1 cup cold water
- 3 tablespoons strawberry gelatin mix
- 1 quart fresh strawberries, drained and sliced
- 1 (9-inch) baked pie crust or crumb crust

• • • • • • • • • • •

Combine sugar and cornstarch, mixing well, and then add cold water; stir to blend. Cook over medium heat until clear. Remove from heat. Add gelatin mix and a drop or two of red food coloring if desired. Add strawberries and mix to coat evenly. Pour mixture into crust. Garnish with whipped topping or vanilla ice cream.

MAKES 8 SERVINGS

PIES & CRUSTS

Squash Pie

1-3/4 cups cooked, strained and mashed butternut or similar kind of squash
1 teaspoon salt
1-1/2 cups milk
3 eggs

1 cup sugar
1 teaspoon cinnamon
1/2 teaspoon nutmeg
1/2 teaspoon ginger
1 tablespoon butter, melted
1 (9-inch) unbaked pie crust

• • • • • • • • • • •

Combine all ingredients except the pie crust and mix well. Pour mixture into crust. Bake at 425 degrees F for 45 to 55 minutes. Check with knife for doneness.

Note: This is very much like pumpkin pie but not as strong. If using another type of squash, drain well after mashing.

MAKES 6 TO 8 SERVINGS

PIES & CRUSTS

Mock Pecan Pie

- 1 cup firmly packed brown sugar
- 3/4 cups sugar
- 2 eggs, beaten
- 1 teaspoon vanilla
- 2 tablespoons butter, softened
- 3/4 cup quick-cooking oats
- 2/3 cup coconut
- 1 (9-inch) unbaked pie crust

Mix sugars, eggs, vanilla and butter together. Stir in oats and coconut. Pour mixture into crust. Bake at 350 degrees F for 35 to 40 minutes, or until set in the middle to knife test.

Makes 8 servings

> This is more from the lean years. It had lots of oats and oatmeal, but no pecans.

PIES & CRUSTS

Pecan Pie

3 eggs
2/3 cup sugar
1/2 teaspoon salt
1 cup dark corn syrup or
   maple syrup

1/2 cup butter, melted
1 cup pecans, chopped
1 (9-inch) unbaked pie crust

• • • • • • • • • • • • •

Combine eggs and sugar; add salt, syrup and butter. Mix well with a hand mixer, and then add pecans. Pour mixture into crust. Bake at 375 degrees F for 40 to 50 minutes, or until center is set.

Makes 6 to 8 servings

> *My mom was ...*
> *the pecan pie queen in our family, but she turned it over to me along with this recipe, making me the pecan pie queen for many years. I have turned the recipe and title over to my daughter. She now reigns over the entire majesty of our family, with the next queen waiting in the wings for the recipe and title.*

PIES & CRUSTS

Pumpkin Pie

3 to 4 egg yolks
1-3/4 cups milk
1-3/4 cups pumpkin, cooked or canned
1 teaspoon salt
2/3 cup firmly packed brown sugar

2 tablespoons sugar
1-1/4 teaspoons cinnamon
1/2 teaspoon ginger
1/2 teaspoon nutmeg
1/2 teaspoon cloves
1 (9-inch) unbaked pie crust

• • • • • • • • • • •

Beat egg yolks, and then add milk and pumpkin. In a separate bowl, combine salt, sugars, cinnamon, ginger, nutmeg and cloves; add to pumpkin mixture. Pour mixture into crust. Bake at 400 degrees F for 45 to 55 minutes, or until done to knife test in center.

Makes 8 servings

PIES & CRUSTS

Mock Apple Pie

2 cups water
2 cups sugar
2 teaspoons cream of tartar
2 tablespoons lemon juice
Grated rind of one lemon

36 Ritz crackers
2 (9-inch) unbaked pie crusts
Butter or margarine
Cinnamon

• • • • • • • • • • • •

Combine water, sugar and cream of tartar in a saucepan. Boil gently for 15 minutes. Add lemon juice and rind; cool. Coarsely break crackers into pastry-lined pie plate. Pour syrup over crackers, dot generously with butter or margarine and sprinkle with cinnamon. Cover with top crust. Trim and flute edges together. Cut slits in top crust to let steam escape. Bake at 450 degrees F for 30 to 35 minutes, or until crust is crisp and golden. Serve hot or cold with vanilla ice cream.

Makes 8 servings

> This recipe comes from the make-do time. Mom could make almost anything out of one kind of cracker or another.

PIES & CRUSTS

Hot Fruit Cobbler

1 cup flour
1 cup sugar
3 tablespoons baking powder

1 cup milk
About 4 cups fruit, peeled and sweetened to taste
1/4 cup margarine, melted

• • • • • • • • • • • •

Spray a 9 x 13-inch baking dish with cooking spray. Combine the flour, sugar and baking powder. Pour into baking dish; add milk and stir to mix. Heat fruit in a saucepan, and then pour evenly over flour mixture. Pour melted margarine over top. Do not stir. Bake at 350 degrees F for about 40 to 45 minutes.

Makes 15 servings

Crumb Crust

1-1/3 cups crushed vanilla wafers

1/4 cup butter, melted

• • • • • • • • • • • •

Mix ingredients together, and then press firmly into a 9-inch pie plate. Bake at 350 degrees F for 12 to 15 minutes, or until lightly brown.

Makes 8 servings

PIES & CRUSTS

Flaky Pie Crust

2-1/4 cups flour
1 teaspoon salt

3/4 cup shortening
About 1/2 cup cold milk

• • • • • • • • • • • •

Blend flour and salt together. Cut shortening into flour mixture with a pastry blender or two forks. When coarse and crumbly, start adding a tablespoon of milk at a time, stirring with a fork until a ball of dough forms. Divide in half. Roll out each half on floured surface to a 12-inch circle and to thickness desired for type of pie.

MAKES 2 PIE CRUSTS

Pie Crust

1 cup plus 2 tablespoons flour
1/2 teaspoon salt
7 tablespoons shortening

About 1/2 cup ice-cold milk
(enough to make sticky dough)

• • • • • • • • • • • •

Mix flour and salt. Cut shortening into flour mixture with a pastry blender or two forks until crumbly. Sprinkle a tablespoon of milk at a time, mixing until dough forms a medium sticky ball. Roll out on a floured board to desired thickness to fit a 9-inch pie or cobbler pan, about a 12-inch circle.

MAKES 1 PIE OR COBBLER CRUST

Cookies

COOKIES

TIPS & HINTS FOR COOKIES

- Run the bottom of a cookie sheet upside down in cold water if using a sheet for more than one batch. This will reduce the chance of burning cookies.

- Don't place cookies on a hot baking sheet. They will lose their shape.

- Remove cookies from the oven a few minutes before they are finished cooking; the hot pan will continue to bake them. This will avoid overbaking.

- Lightly toast oatmeal before making oatmeal cookies to add a crunchy texture. Sprinkle the oatmeal in a thin layer on a baking sheet and toast at 185 degrees F for 10 to 15 minutes, or until lightly browned.

- Roll sugar cookies in sugar instead of flour for cookies that aren't stiff or tough.

COOKIES

- Keep crisp cookies in a cookie can with a loose cover to retain their crispness.

- Store soft cookies in a tightly sealed container with half an apple or a slice of bread to keep them moist. Change the apple or bread frequently.

- Package cookies for shipping with popped popcorn.

- Chilling cookie dough for 10 to 15 minutes before rolling will stop the dough from sticking to the rolling pin.

- Crisp cookies that have become soft by placing them in a 275-degree F oven for 5 minutes.

- Make sure baking soda, baking powder and cream of tartar are not old. One year is the limit for real freshness.

COOKIES

Kookie Brittle

- 1 cup margarine, softened
- 1-1/2 teaspoons vanilla
- 1 teaspoon salt
- 1 cup sugar
- 2 cups flour
- 1 (6-ounce) package chocolate chips
- 3/4 cup nuts, chopped

• • • • • • • • • • • •

Combine the margarine, vanilla and salt using a hand mixer; beat in the sugar. Add flour, chocolate chips and nuts; mix well. Press evenly into an ungreased cookie sheet. Bake at 375 degrees F for 25 minutes, or until golden brown. Cool, and then break into irregular pieces like brittle.

Makes about 3 dozen pieces

COOKIES

Date Bars

- 2 eggs
- 1 cup sugar
- 1 cup vegetable oil
- 1 cup flour
- 1 teaspoon baking powder
- 1/2 teaspoon salt
- 1 cup chopped dates
- 1/2 cup walnuts or pecans, chopped

• • • • • • • • • • • •

Beat eggs, and then add sugar, oil, flour, baking powder and salt. Stir in dates and nuts. Pour into a greased and floured 8 x 10-inch baking pan. Bake at 350 degrees F for 20 to 30 minutes, and then cool slightly, until it can be handled. Cut into squares and roll each square in powdered sugar while still warm.

Makes 12 servings

COOKIES

Crisp Sugar Drop Cookies

2-1/2 cups flour
1/2 teaspoon baking soda
1 teaspoon salt
1 egg, slightly beaten
2 tablespoons white vinegar
1-1/2 teaspoons grated lemon rind

1 teaspoon vanilla
1/2 cup margarine, softened
1/2 cup shortening
1 cup sugar, plus more to sprinkle

• • • • • • • • • • • •

Combine flour, baking soda and salt; set aside. Combine egg, vinegar, lemon rind and vanilla; set aside. Cream margarine and shortening, and then add sugar gradually. Add dry mixture alternately with egg mixture. Drop dough by spoonfuls onto an ungreased cookie sheet; flatten with a floured fork, and then sprinkle with sugar. Bake at 400 degrees F for 10 to 12 minutes. Cool on a wire rack.

Makes 5 dozen cookies

COOKIES

Oatmeal Drop Cookies

1/2 cup shortening, softened
1-1/4 cups sugar
2 eggs, slightly beaten
6 tablespoons molasses
1-2/3 cups flour

1 teaspoon baking soda
1 teaspoon salt
1 teaspoon cinnamon
2 cups rolled oats
1/2 cup nuts, chopped
1 cup raisins, chopped

Quick Cream Icing
3/4 cup powdered sugar
1/4 teaspoon vanilla
1/2 teaspoon milk

• • • • • • • • • • •

Combine shortening, sugar, eggs and molasses. In a separate bowl, sift together flour, baking soda, salt, and cinnamon. Mix into the molasses mixture. Stir in the oats, nuts and raisins. Drop dough by rounded teaspoonfuls about 2 inches apart on a lightly greased cookie sheet. Bake at 400 degrees F for 8 to 10 minutes, or until lightly browned.

Quick Cream Icing

Blend powdered sugar, vanilla and milk together; cream until spreadable. May need to add a drop more milk, being careful not to make it too thin.

MAKES 3 DOZEN COOKIES

COOKIES

Potato Chip Cookies

1 cup butter or margarine
3/4 cup sugar
2 cups flour

1/2 cup nuts, chopped
1/2 cup crumbled potato chips

• • • • • • • • • • • •

Cream butter and sugar together, and then add remaining ingredients. Form dough into balls, and then mash with fork on the cookie sheet. Bake at 350 degrees F for 15 minutes.

Makes 2 dozen cookies

COOKIES

Soft Molasses Cookies

4-1/2 cups flour
1 teaspoon baking soda
2 teaspoons baking powder
3 teaspoons ground ginger
1 cup butter or shortening
1 cup firmly packed light brown sugar

2 eggs, beaten
3/4 cup molasses
3/4 cup sour milk
2 teaspoons vanilla

• • • • • • • • • • •

Sift flour, baking soda, baking powder and ginger together three times. Cream butter, eggs and molasses, and then slowly beat in sugar. Add flour mixture alternately with milk and vanilla, beating after each addition, and then chill 2 to 3 hours. On a lightly floured board, roll out dough to 1/8 inch thickness, cut with cookie cutter and sprinkle with a little sugar. Bake at 375 degrees F for about 12 minutes.

MAKES 8 DOZEN COOKIES

COOKIES

Corn Flake Cookies

2 cups flour
1 teaspoon baking soda
1/2 teaspoon salt
1/2 teaspoon baking powder
1 cup shortening
1 cup sugar

1 cup firmly packed brown sugar
2 eggs, well beaten
1 teaspoon vanilla
2 cups coconut
2 cups corn flakes

• • • • • • • • • • •

Mix together flour, baking soda, salt and baking powder. Cream shortening, and then add sugars gradually; beat until light. Add eggs and vanilla. Combine flour mixture and creamed mixture. Stir in coconut and corn flakes. Drop by small teaspoonfuls on a greased baking sheet. Bake at 350 degrees F for 8 to 10 minutes, or until delicately brown.

MAKES ABOUT 8 DOZEN COOKIES

COOKIES

Caramel Corn

16 cups popped popcorn
1 cup firmly packed brown sugar
1/2 cup dark corn syrup

1/2 cup butter
1/2 teaspoon salt
1 teaspoon vanilla
1/2 teaspoon baking soda

• • • • • • • • • •

Pick out any kernels of corn that did not pop. Place popcorn in a large bowl and set aside. Combine brown sugar, syrup, butter and salt in a 3- to 4-quart saucepan; cook over medium heat, stirring constantly, bringing to a boil. Cook 5 minutes without stirring, remove from heat, and then stir in vanilla and baking soda, mixing well. Pour over popcorn, stirring to coat evenly. Pour popcorn into an 11 x 13-inch baking pan. Bake at 250 degrees F for 60 minutes, stirring a couple of times. Cool, crumble and store in an airtight container.

Makes 8 servings

Breads

BREADS

TIPS & HINTS FOR BREADS

- Gently add yeast to water, but never add water to yeast.

- Dry yeast will stay fresh longer if stored in the refrigerator.

- Bake biscuits on sheets without sides; heat circulates more evenly.

- Biscuits touching each other will make a moister and heavier biscuit.

- Baking biscuits on a cookie sheet makes them crusty and crumbly.

- Double the yeast called for in a recipe to cut rising time by about 1 hour without changing the taste of the bread.

- It is easier to knead dough that is placed in a plastic bag.

- Be sure to bring any baking ingredients, such as yeast, butter and eggs, to room temperature before using.

- Cool freshly baked bread on a wire rack to keep it from becoming soggy.

BREADS

- To keep the bread crust from becoming too hard, place a pan of water in the oven while baking. The moisture and steam will do the trick.

- Moldy bread should be thrown out even if only one slice in the package has mold.

- Quick breads use baking powder or baking soda in place of the yeast.

- Don't scrub bread pans until they are shiny because bread will bake better in a dull pan.

- When freezing bread, place a paper towel in the container. It will keep the bread from becoming mushy when it is thawed.

BREADS

Banana Bread

1/2 cup butter
1 cup sugar
3 bananas, mashed
2 eggs

2 cups flour
1/2 teaspoon salt
1 teaspoon baking soda
1 cup nuts, chopped

• • • • • • • • • • •

Cream butter, sugar, bananas and eggs together; add remaining ingredients. Bake in two small 7-inch greased and floured loaf pans at 350 degrees F for 45 to 50 minutes. Check for doneness with a toothpick.

Makes 8 servings

BREADS

Biscuits

2 cups flour
3 teaspoons baking powder
1 teaspoon sugar

1/2 teaspoon salt
4 tablespoons shortening
3/4 cup milk

• • • • • • • • • • •

Combine all of the dry ingredients in a bowl. Cut in shortening with a pastry blender or two forks until evenly mixed or crumbly. Add milk and stir slightly until dough is puffy and moist. Turn out onto a floured board and knead five to six times; pat out to about 1/2-inch thickness and cut into biscuits with a biscuit cutter. Bake in a greased 8 x 10-inch pan at 400 degrees F. for 10 to 12 minutes.

MAKES 8 BISCUITS

BREADS

No Knead Bread

- 1 package dry yeast
- 1/4 cup hot tap water (not boiling)
- 2-1/2 cups flour, divided
- 1-1/2 tablespoons sugar
- 1/4 teaspoon baking soda
- 1 teaspoon salt
- 3/4 cup sour cream
- 2 eggs

• • • • • • • • • • •

In a glass or metal bowl, dissolve yeast in water. In a separate bowl mix 1-1/2 cups flour with sugar, baking soda and salt; stir to blend. With a hand mixer, add flour mixture to yeast mixture along with sour cream and eggs, mixing on low speed for about 1 minute. Continue to mix on high speed for 2 minutes more, scraping bowl occasionally. Stir in remaining flour by hand. Divide batter evenly into lightly greased muffin cups. Let rise in a warm place for about 50 minutes. (Batter will rise somewhat but will not double in size.) Bake at 350 degrees F for 30 minutes, or until golden brown. Immediately remove from pan, and then brush tops with soft butter.

MAKES 6 SERVINGS

Note: This can be made the night before. Cover dough with plastic wrap sprayed with cooking spray or greased wax paper and refrigerate for 6 to 24 hours before use. Remove from refrigerator 3 to 4 hours before baking. This is a one-bowl mix with mixer—easy bread.

BREADS

Cornbread

2 tablespoons oil or grease
2 cups yellow cornmeal
1 teaspoon baking soda
1/2 teaspoon salt
1/2 teaspoon baking powder

1-1/2 tablespoons flour
2 eggs
1-1/2 to 2 cups buttermilk, divided

• • • • • • • • • • •

Place oil or grease into a cast-iron skillet, and then place skillet in oven to heat while mixing bread batter. If using an 8 x 8-inch baking dish instead of a skillet, just spray with cooking oil or add oil and coat evenly; set aside.

Mix dry ingredients together, make a well in the center, and then add eggs and half the buttermilk. Stir and continue adding buttermilk until desired consistency or a thick pourable batter. If too thick, add a little water. Pour into prepared pan, bake at 375 degrees F for about 45 to 60 minutes for skillet, or about 45 to 50 minutes for 8 x 8-inch dish. If using a cast-iron skillet, when done, flip out onto plate, crusty side up. Cut into wedges. Looks just like Grandma did it, doesn't it?

MAKES 5 TO 6 SERVINGS

BREADS

English Muffin Casserole Bread

2-1/2 to 3 cups flour, divided
1 package active dry yeast
1-1/4 cups water

1 tablespoon sugar
3/4 tablespoon salt
Cornmeal

• • • • • • • • • • •

Combine 1 cup flour and yeast. Heat water, sugar and salt in a saucepan just until warm, stirring to dissolve sugar. Add to flour mixture. Beat at low speed with a hand mixer for 30 seconds. Beat on high speed 3 minutes. By hand, stir in enough remaining flour to make a soft dough; shape into a ball. Place dough ball in a lightly greased bowl and turn once. Cover and let rise until double in size, about 1 hour; punch down. Cover and let rest for 10 minutes. Grease a 1-quart casserole dish, transfer dough to dish and sprinkle with cornmeal; cover and let rise until double in size, about 30 to 40 minutes. Bake in dish at 400 degrees F for 40 to 45 minutes. Cover loosely with foil if top browns too quickly.

MAKES 8 SERVINGS

BREADS

Old-Fashioned Oatmeal Bread

- 1 package dry yeast
- 1/4 cup lukewarm water
- 1/2 cup scalded milk
- 1/2 cup shortening
- 1/3 cup sugar
- 1 teaspoon salt
- 2 eggs
- 3 to 3-1/2 cups flour, divided
- 1 cup oats, quick or old-fashioned, uncooked
- Melted shortening

• • • • • • • • • • • •

Dissolve yeast in water. Pour milk over shortening, and then add sugar and salt; cool to lukewarm. Beat in eggs, yeast mixture, 2 cups flour and oats. Stir in more flour, enough to make a soft dough. Turn out onto lightly floured board and knead until satiny, about 10 minutes. Round dough into ball. Place in a greased bowl, and then brush lightly with melted shortening. Cover and let rise until double in size, about 1 to 1-1/2 hours; punch dough down, and then turn out onto a lightly floured board. Cover and let rest 10 minutes.

Divide dough in half and knead each half until dough is smooth. Place into greased loaf pans. Cover with plastic wrap lightly sprayed with cooking spray; let rise until bread is well rounded over top of pans. Bake at 350 degrees F for about 20 to 25 minutes. Butter tops.

Makes 2 loaves

BREADS

Refrigerator Rolls

2 packages dry active yeast
2 cups warm water
1/2 cup sugar
2 teaspoons salt

6 to 7 cups flour, divided
1 egg
1/4 cup shortening

• • • • • • • • • • • •

In a large metal or glass bowl, dissolve yeast in water; let set 10 minutes. Mix sugar, salt and half the flour in a separate bowl. Add flour mixture to the yeast mixture, beating thoroughly. Add egg and shortening; beat well. Add remaining flour, small amounts at a time, until dough is easy to handle. Place in a greased bowl and turn over, leaving greased side up. Cover with plastic wrap and refrigerate until needed, punching down as dough rises. About 2 to 2-1/2 hours before baking time, cut off amount needed and return remaining dough to refrigerator. Shape into rolls while cold, and then place in well-greased baking pans. Cover; let rise until double in size. Bake at 375 degrees F for 12 to 15 minutes. Butter tops of rolls when removed from oven.

MAKES 4 DOZEN ROLLS

Note: This is a large recipe, so you can have dough on hand. Will keep 4 to 5 days in the refrigerator. Good for making ahead to entertain.

BREADS

Soda Biscuits

2 cups flour
3/4 teaspoon baking soda
1/2 teaspoon salt

1/4 cup shortening
1/4 cup distilled vinegar
1/2 cup milk

• • • • • • • • • • •

Sift together flour, baking soda and salt; cut in shortening. Add vinegar to milk and then stir slightly. (May substitute 3/4 cup buttermilk for vinegar and milk.) Add to flour mixture, stirring until dough is sticky. Turn onto a floured board and knead lightly. Roll out to about 1/2-inch thickness, cut biscuits and place on a greased baking sheet or into greased pans. Bake at 450 degrees F for 12 to 15 minutes, or until browned.

Makes 12 to 16 servings

BREADS

Sweet Roll Dough

1/2 cup warm water
2 packages dry yeast
1-1/2 cups sugar
2 teaspoons salt

7 to 7-1/2 cups flour, divided
1-1/2 cups lukewarm milk
2 eggs
1/2 cup shortening, softened

• • • • • • • • • • • •

Mix water and yeast together and let stand 5 minutes. Combine sugar, salt and half the flour; mix. Add milk, eggs and shortening. Stir to mix, and then add yeast mixture. Mix well; add remaining flour, small amounts at a time. Turn onto a floured board, knead 3 to 4 minutes and place in bowl; let rest 10 minutes. Shape into rolls and bake at 350 degrees F for 20 to 25 minutes, or until golden brown. Or roll out on a floured board to form doughnuts or cinnamon rolls.

Doughnuts
Roll to about 3/4-inch thickness; cut out doughnuts and deep fry. Drain and roll in sugar.

Cinnamon Rolls
Roll to 3/4-inch thickness, spread with 1/2 cup softened butter. Mix 1 cup sugar with 1 teaspoon cinnamon, and then sprinkle over butter; roll dough from long side to long side. Cut rolls with a sharp knife, and then place in a well-greased baking pan and bake at 350 degrees F for 25 to 35 minutes. Drizzle with a powdered sugar glaze or sprinkle with additional sugar and cinnamon mixture. Add pecans if desired.

MAKES 12 SERVINGS

BREADS

Yeast Rolls

1 package dry yeast
1 cup warm water
1 cup scalded milk
5 tablespoons sugar

1 teaspoon salt
3 to 4 cups flour
6 tablespoons shortening

• • • • • • • • • • •

Dissolve yeast in water. Scald milk and add sugar and salt; cool milk to warm, and then add yeast mixture. Beat in 3 cups flour, mixing well; beat in shortening. Add enough flour to make medium round dough. Place in a greased or oiled glass or metal bowl, cover with plastic wrap and let rise until double in size. (I use cupcake pans, placing two medium rolls or three smaller rolls in each, which makes the old-fashioned clover leaf roll.) Bake at 350 degrees F for about 25 to 30 minutes, or until desired doneness. Butter tops when taken out of oven.

Makes 8 to 10 servings

BREADS

Corn Dodgers

1-1/2 cups white cornmeal
1 teaspoon salt

About 2 cups boiling water
2-1/2 cups cooking oil

• • • • • • • • • • •

In a glass or metal mixing bowl, combine cornmeal and salt. Start pouring the boiling water into the cornmeal mixture, stirring constantly. Start with about 2 cups water, but be careful to add a small amount at a time. When the mixture is very thick, but pliable, cover with a cloth or plastic wrap and let stand for 10 minutes. Shape dough into balls, about 1-1/2 inches, and then flatten slightly. Place on a dish and cover until ready to fry. Heat oil, about 1-1/2 inches deep in skillet. When very hot, fry a single layer of corn dodgers until lightly browned on the bottom side, turning carefully, frying until brown on the other side. Remove from grease and drain on paper towels. Split if desired, butter and eat. Yum!

Makes 6 to 8 servings

BREADS

Corn Sticks

1/3 cup flour
1/2 teaspoon salt
1 teaspoon baking powder
1/2 teaspoon baking soda
1 tablespoon sugar

1-1/3 cups yellow cornmeal
1 egg, beaten
1 cup buttermilk
2 tablespoons shortening, melted

• • • • • • • • • • • •

Mix flour, salt, baking powder, baking soda, sugar and cornmeal together. Add the egg, buttermilk and shortening; mix well. Pour into a well-greased corn stick pan. Bake at 400 degrees F for 25 to 30 minutes.

Makes 12 to 14 servings

> *Remember the old . . .*
> cast-iron corn stick pans? After I grew up, I loved going to restaurants that made these corn sticks in those pans. Mom didn't have one of the pans that makes them so cute and crusty, nor did she have the time to "mess" with them.

BREADS

Curt's English Muffins

1 cup scalded milk
1/4 cup shortening
2 teaspoons salt
1 tablespoon plus 1 teaspoon sugar, divided

1 package dry yeast
1/4 cup warm water
3 cups flour
Cornmeal

• • • • • • • • • • •

Combine milk, shortening, salt and 1 tablespoon sugar; cool to lukewarm. Dissolve yeast and 1 teaspoon sugar in the water; let stand 10 minutes. Add yeast mixture to milk mixture. Add flour and mix until well blended. Roll out dough on a floured board to 1/4-inch thickness. Cut out with English muffin cutter or large biscuit cutter. Sprinkle cornmeal on an ungreased baking sheet. Place muffins on baking sheet and then sprinkle tops with cornmeal; let rise for about 1 hour. Cook muffins on a hot griddle or electric skillet (like pancakes) at 340 degrees F for about 5 minutes, turning when half done; split each muffin.

MAKES 6 SERVINGS

Note: These muffins freeze well and are great reheated in the toaster.

Breakfast

BREAKFAST

Ham and Cheese Breakfast Casserole

6 crescent rolls
1 (8-ounce) package whipped cream cheese
6 slices ham
8 eggs
1/2 cup sugar

1/2 cup cream
1 tablespoon flour
1 teaspoon almond extract
1/2 cup orange marmalade
1/4 cup orange juice

• • • • • • • • • • •

Split rolls, and then spread a layer of cream cheese and a slice of ham on each side and put rolls back together. Place rolls in a greased 9 x 12-inch pan. Beat eggs, sugar, cream and flour together. Pour mixture over rolls. Mix almond extract, marmalade and orange juice together and then spread over rolls and refrigerate overnight. Bake at 350 degrees F for 30 minutes.

Makes 6 servings

BREAKFAST

Muffins

1 egg
1 cup milk
1/4 cup vegetable oil
2 cups flour

1/2 cup sugar
2 teaspoons baking powder
1 teaspoon salt

• • • • • • • • • • • •

Beat egg, and then stir in milk and oil. Blend flour, sugar, baking powder and salt in a bowl. Mix flour mixture into milk mixture, and then stir just enough to moisten. Spoon batter into a lightly sprayed muffin pan. Bake at 400 degrees F for 20 to 25 minutes.

Makes 12 muffins

BREAKFAST

Pancake or Waffle Batter

1 cup flour
1 teaspoon baking powder
1/2 teaspoon baking soda
1/4 teaspoon salt

1 egg
1 cup buttermilk
3 tablespoons shortening, at room temperature

• • • • • • • • • • • •

Combine flour, baking powder, baking soda and salt. Add the egg, buttermilk and shortening; mix until smooth. Pour about 1/4 cup batter for each pancake onto hot griddle and cook until bubbly; turn over and cook until center springs back when touched. For waffles, pour desired amount of batter into a waffle iron and cook until lightly toasted.

MAKES 8 SERVINGS

BREAKFAST

Omelet

6 eggs, separated
6 scant teaspoons cornstarch
1 cup milk
1/2 teaspoon salt
1 teaspoon baking powder
Pepper to taste

Dash of paprika
Cheese and/or cooked ham, cut into bite-size pieces
2 to 3 tablespoons butter, melted

• • • • • • • • • • •

Beat egg yolks, add cornstarch dissolved in a little of the milk, and then add remaining milk and salt. Beat egg whites stiff with a hand mixer, adding baking powder as you beat them. Blend egg mixtures together; add pepper, paprika, cheese and/or ham. Pour into a hot cast-iron or ovenproof skillet with melted butter and bake at 350 degrees F for 20 to 30 minutes.

Makes 4 servings

Note: Chopped crisp bacon, peppers, onions or mushrooms may also be added if desired.

BREAKFAST

Chocolate Gravy

2 cups sugar
4 tablespoons cocoa
1 tablespoon flour

1/2 cup milk
3 to 4 eggs
2 tablespoons butter

• • • • • • • • • • • • •

Mix the sugar, cocoa and flour together; add remaining ingredients except butter. Cook, stirring constantly to keep from sticking, until thick. (Will have the consistency of pudding.) Remove from heat, add butter and stir to blend. Serve over hot biscuits.

Makes 6 servings

BREAKFAST

Breakfast Casserole

6 slices bread, cubed (about 3/4-inch cubes)
1 pound sausage, bacon or ham (or a combination), cooked and crumbled
1 cup grated cheddar cheese
8 eggs, slightly beaten
2 cups milk
1 teaspoon salt
1 teaspoon dry mustard

• • • • • • • • • • •

Place bread cubes in a 2- to 3-quart buttered baking dish, and then sprinkle meat over bread. Sprinkle cheese over meat. Mix eggs, milk, salt and dry mustard together, and then pour over bread and meat mixture. Cover and refrigerate overnight. Bake at 350 degrees F for 35 minutes.

Makes 6 to 8 servings

BREAKFAST

Oatmeal Pancakes

1-1/2 cups oats
1 tablespoon baking powder
2 tablespoons flour

2 egg whites
1-1/4 cups milk
1 tablespoon vegetable oil

• • • • • • • • • • •

Put oats, baking powder and flour in a blender and blend until it reaches a flour consistency. Beat egg whites until foamy; add milk, oil and oatmeal mixture, and let stand for 5 minutes. Pour about 1/4 cup batter for each pancake onto hot griddle or hot skillet sprayed lightly with cooking spray until bubbly; flip and brown the other side.

Makes 12 medium-size pancakes

BREAKFAST

French Toast

2 eggs
1/2 teaspoon salt
1 tablespoon sugar

1/4 cup milk
6 slices thick bread
Butter, margarine or bacon drippings for frying

• • • • • • • • • • • •

Mix eggs, salt, sugar and milk in a shallow dish. Dip bread in, turning to coat, and then fry both sides in a hot skillet. Serve with maple syrup.

Makes 6 slices

BREAKFAST

Overnight French Toast

8 slices (3/4-inch thick) French bread
4 eggs
1 cup milk

1 tablespoon sugar
1/2 teaspoon vanilla
1/4 teaspoon cinnamon

• • • • • • • • • • •

Place bread in a lightly buttered 9 x 13-inch baking dish. Combine eggs, milk, sugar, vanilla and cinnamon; beat well. Pour mixture over the bread and turn each slice to coat evenly. Cover and refrigerate up to 8 hours. Heat nonstick skillet or griddle slightly sprayed with cooking spray to medium-hot. Fry until lightly browned on each side, turning once.

Makes 8 slices

Salads

SALADS

TIPS & HINTS FOR SALADS

- Potatoes are available year-round and should be smooth and well shaped when purchasing them.

- Do not buy potatoes if they have already sprouted or if the skins have a greenish tint because they may be hazardous to eat.

- Store potatoes at room temperature in a dark area; do not refrigerate.

- Oil or butter a potato instead of wrapping it in foil for baking. It will bake faster.

- A potato will bake faster if it is soaked in hot water for a few minutes before baking.

SALADS

Shoepeg Corn Salad

1 (11-ounce) can shoepeg corn, drained
1 (15-ounce) can English or green peas, drained
1 (15-ounce) can lima beans, drained
1 green bell pepper, chopped
1/2 cup chopped red onion
1/2 cup chopped celery

Marinade
1/2 cup apple cider vinegar
1/2 cup vegetable oil
3/4 cup sugar
Salt and pepper to taste

• • • • • • • • • • •

Pour all vegetables in a bowl and set aside.

Marinade
Combine all marinade ingredients in a small bowl, and then pour over vegetables and stir. Refrigerate vegetables in marinade overnight. Keeps for several days. Drain to serve.

Makes 8 to 10 servings

SALADS

Cornbread Salad

2 (6-ounce) packages yellow cornbread mix
1 large green bell pepper, chopped fine (about 1 cup)
1 large onion, chopped fine (about 2 cups)
1 large tomato, chopped
1 teaspoon seasoning salt
2 cups Miracle Whip

• • • • • • • • • • •

Cook cornbread mixes according to package directions, and then cool and crumble. Add bell pepper, onion, tomato and salt. Fold in Miracle Whip, and then it is ready to eat!

Makes 6 servings

SALADS

Macaroni Salad

- 1 (8-ounce) package macaroni, any style or shape will work
- 1 large tomato, diced
- 3/4 cup chopped onion
- 3/4 cup chopped green bell pepper
- 3/4 cup sliced pimiento-stuffed green olives
- 1 cup mayonnaise
- Salt and pepper to taste

• • • • • • • • • • •

Cook macaroni according to package directions; drain, rinse in cold water, and then drain again. Combine all ingredients, adding mayonnaise 1/2 cup at a time, stirring to coat.

Makes 6 to 8 servings

> Mom was the . . .
> macaroni salad queen in the area. She would take it to dinners, especially during the summer when we had tomatoes and peppers available, since we lived in a rural area with a small country store that didn't offer refrigeration or fresh vegetables. It was always on our table for holidays during the later years, after we moved to town.

SALADS

Potato Salad

- 6 to 8 potatoes, peeled, cut into 1-1/2-inch chunks, boiled until tender and, drained
- 4 to 5 hard-boiled eggs, peeled

- 3/4 cup finely chopped dill pickles
- 1/2 to 3/4 cup finely chopped onion

Dressing
- 3/4 to 1 cup mayonnaise
- 3 to 4 tablespoons mustard
- 1 tablespoon vegetable oil
- 1 tablespoon vinegar
- Pinch of salt
- Pepper to taste

• • • • • • • • • • •

Combine hot potatoes and eggs. Mash with a potato masher to an almost smooth consistency resembling mashed potatoes. (Use a hand mixer if desired, but it creates a different texture.) Add pickles and onion.

Dressing
Combine all ingredients in a bowl, and then add to potato mixture; mix well. Taste and make adjustments as to moisture and add additional mayonnaise, mustard, salt or pepper, if necessary.

Makes 6 to 8 servings

> This is an old-fashioned . . .
> potato salad recipe. I stood in a chair beside my Grandmother Sloan and watched her make this so many times. I have the old aluminum pot she used to make it in. She made it with the dabbler method—a dab of this, a dab of that. My son tells me I'm a dabbler cook too.

SALADS

Chicken Salad

4 chicken breasts halves, cooked and chopped
1 cup chopped celery
1 cup chopped sweet pickles
3 to 4 hard-boiled eggs, peeled and chopped
1 large apple, peeled and chopped
3/4 cup pecans, chopped
3/4 cup mayonnaise
Salt and pepper to taste

• • • • • • • • • • •

Combine all ingredients together in a bowl. Add enough mayonnaise to make as moist as you desire. Make sandwiches on toasted bread or serve salad stuffed in a tomato cut into fourths or on a crescent roll sandwich.

Makes 6 to 8 servings

SALADS

Strawberry Gelatin Salad

2 cups cola, heated
1 (3-ounce) box
   strawberry gelatin
1 (8-ounce) can pineapple
   chunks, drained
1 (10-ounce) jar
   maraschino cherries,
   drained and chopped
1 cup nuts, chopped
1 (8-ounce) package cold, firm
   cream cheese, grated

• • • • • • • • • • •

Pour cola over gelatin and mix until dissolved. Add pineapple, cherries, nuts and cream cheese; mix well. Pour into an 8 x 12-inch baking dish and refrigerate until set.

Makes 8 servings

SALADS

Chunky Potato Salad

4 to 5 large potatoes, boiled, cooled and cut into chunks
1 cup chopped onion
3/4 cup chopped sweet pickles

3 to 4 hard-boiled eggs, peeled and chopped

Dressing

1 cup mayonnaise
2 to 3 tablespoons mustard
2 to 3 tablespoons pickle juice
Splash of vinegar (about 2 teaspoons)
1 teaspoon vegetable oil
Pinch of salt
Dash of pepper

• • • • • • • • • • •

Combine all salad ingredients in a bowl; set aside.

Dressing
Combine all dressing ingredients in a bowl, and then stir into salad and toss to coat evenly. Refrigerate at least 1 hour before serving.

MAKES 8 TO 10 SERVINGS

Note: To do ahead, layer salad ingredients in a bowl, potatoes on top; do not stir—just cover and refrigerate. Mix dressing ingredients together and then cover and store. Combine salad and dressing and toss to coat evenly at least 1 hour before serving.

SALADS

One-Cup Salad

1 cup mandarin oranges, drained
1 cup coconut

1 cup crushed pineapple, drained
1 cup small marshmallows
1 cup sour cream

• • • • • • • • • • •

Mix all ingredients together in a bowl and chill. Easy!

Makes 4 to 6 servings

SALADS

Layered Salad

- 1 head lettuce, shredded
- 1/2 cup chopped celery
- 1/2 cup chopped green bell peppers
- 1 medium onion, thinly sliced or ringed, or use sliced green onions
- 1 (16-ounce) package frozen green peas, not thawed
- 2 cups mayonnaise
- 1 tablespoon sugar
- 8 slices bacon, cooked and crumbled
- 1/2 cup grated cheddar cheese

• • • • • • • • • • •

Arrange first 5 ingredients in layers as listed. Smooth mayonnaise to edges of salad, and then sprinkle last 3 ingredients evenly over top. Do not stir! Cover with foil or plastic wrap and refrigerate overnight. Serve from bowl using salad tongs, dipping straight up and down to serve all salad ingredients.

Makes 6 to 8 servings

Note: Use a clear glass bowl or pedestal bowl as this is a very pretty salad.

SALADS

Pink Stuff

- 1 (12-ounce) container frozen whipped topping, thawed
- 1 (14-ounce) can sweetened condensed milk
- 1 (21-ounce) can cherry pie filling
- 1 (20-ounce) can crushed pineapple, with juice
- 1 cup miniature marshmallows
- 1/2 cup coconut
- 1/2 cup nuts, chopped

• • • • • • • • • • • • •

Mix whipped topping and condensed milk together in a bowl. Add remaining ingredients, stir to mix, and then let set overnight.

Makes 8 to 10 servings

> The name Pink Stuff . . .
> comes from our family dinners. For holiday dinners, everyone brought something, usually their special dish. One of the grandsons married during the summer, and at Christmas his new wife brought this salad. It didn't have a name, so our family called it Pink Stuff.

Side Dishes

SIDE DISHES

TIPS & HINTS FOR SPINACH AND ONIONS

- To retain nutrients in spinach, boil it as little as possible and in one cup of water instead of two.

- To squeeze water out of spinach, place spinach in a colander to drain, and then squeeze handfuls of the spinach to remove excess water.

- Onions should be hard and dry. Do not buy onions that have wet necks since this means they are already decaying.

- Avoid onions with sprouts.

- Onions can be stored at room temperature or refrigerated.

- Some ways to get rid of the onion smell from your hands include washing your hands in cold water, and then rubbing them with salt, or rinsing your hands with vinegar.

- If you need only half an onion, cut the top half off; wrap and store the root half in the refrigerator. It will keep fresh longer.

SIDE DISHES

Corn and Rice Casserole

1 medium green bell pepper, chopped
1 large onion, chopped
1/2 cup margarine
1-1/2 cups rice, cooked
2 (15-ounce) cans cream-style corn
1 (4-ounce) jar pimientos, drained and chopped
1 egg, beaten
2 tablespoons sugar
Salt and pepper to taste

• • • • • • • • • • •

Saute bell pepper and onion in margarine in a large skillet. Add rice, mixing well. Add corn, pimientos, egg, sugar, salt and pepper; mix well. Pour mixture into a prepared 9 x 13-inch baking dish. Bake at 350 degrees F for 25 to 35 minutes.

MAKES 8 SERVINGS

SIDE DISHES

Broccoli Casserole

- 1 cup chopped onion
- 3/4 cup diced celery
- 1/4 cup butter or margarine
- 1 (15-ounce) can cream of mushroom soup
- 1 (8-ounce) jar Cheez Whiz
- 1 cup rice, cooked
- 2 (16-ounce) packages (about 4 cups) frozen chopped broccoli, cooked and drained

• • • • • • • • • • • •

Cook onion and celery in butter; add soup, Cheez Whiz, rice and broccoli. Stir until soup and cheese are hot. Pour into a buttered casserole dish and bake at 350 degrees F for 30 to 40 minutes, or until bubbly and lightly browned. Can make day ahead, but do not bake until ready to serve. Cool and store in covered container.

Makes 8 to 10 servings

SIDE DISHES

Quick Fix Cabbage

- 2 slices bacon, cut into small pieces
- 1/2 small onion, chopped (about 1/3 cup)
- 1 medium-size head cabbage, chopped
- 1/2 teaspoon salt
- 1/4 teaspoon dried basil
- 1/4 teaspoon dried oregano
- 1/4 teaspoon dried marjoram
- 1/4 teaspoon black pepper

• • • • • • • • • • •

Cook bacon in a large nonstick skillet over medium heat until crisp. Remove bacon and cook the onion in the drippings. Add cabbage and seasonings. Cook, stirring constantly, about 1 minute. Cover and cook for 2 to 3 minutes. Sprinkle bacon over top and serve immediately.

Makes 6 servings

Note: Cabbage should not be mushy like grandma cooked it. Remember, it was not easy to turn down the heat on a wood stove.

SIDE DISHES

Tomato Pie

1-1/2 cups flour
2 teaspoons baking powder
1/2 teaspoon salt
3 tablespoons butter
2/3 cup milk

4 medium ripe tomatoes
Salt and pepper
1/2 cup grated cheese
3/4 cup mayonnaise

• • • • • • • • • • • •

Sift together flour, baking powder and salt. Cut in butter, and then add milk. Stir quickly until dough forms a ball. Press in the bottom of a greased 9-inch pie pan. Slice tomatoes and arrange in layer over dough, seasoning with salt and pepper. Mix cheese and mayonnaise together, and then spread over tomatoes. Bake at 400 degrees F for 25 to 30 minutes, or until golden brown. Serve hot.

Makes 6 servings

SIDE DISHES

Scalloped Pineapple

1 cup butter
2 cups sugar
3 eggs
2-1/2 (20-ounce) cans crushed pineapple, with liquid

4 cups bread, broken into small pieces
2 tablespoons milk

• • • • • • • • • • • •

Cream butter, and then add sugar. Add remaining ingredients in order listed and stir. Pour mixture into baking pan. Bake at 350 degrees F for 60 minutes in a 9 x 13-inch baking pan that has been lightly sprayed. Can make a day ahead. Mix as directed, store in a covered container and bake when ready.

Makes 12 servings

SIDE DISHES

Candied Sweet Potatoes

4 to 6 sweet potatoes, skins on
3/4 cup firmly packed brown sugar
1/3 cup honey
1/4 cup Coconut Amaretto

Pinch of salt
2 tablespoons sugar
3/4 cup maple syrup
1/4 to 1/2 cup butter, thinly sliced

• • • • • • • • • • •

Wash and boil potatoes to crisp tender (not quite done); cool, peel and cube. Place in buttered casserole dish, and then pour each of remaining ingredients except butter evenly over potatoes. Place butter slices on top. Bake at 350 degrees F for about 30 to 45 minutes, or until fork tender. May add marshmallows and brown if desired.

Variation: Candied Carrots
Make the same using two to three 1-pound bags baby carrots. Can be started raw but may need to cook a little longer.

MAKES 4 SERVINGS

SIDE DISHES

Baked Turnips

5 cups peeled, diced turnips
1 teaspoon salt
1 teaspoon sugar
2 tablespoons butter
2 tablespoons flour
1-1/2 cups milk

1 teaspoon seasoning salt
1/8 teaspoon pepper
3/4 cup grated cheddar cheese
1/4 cup fine dry breadcrumbs

• • • • • • • • • • •

Combine first three ingredients and cook until tender; drain well and set aside. Melt butter in a large heavy saucepan; add flour, stirring constantly. Gradually add milk and cook until thickened. Add remaining ingredients except breadcrumbs and stir until cheese melts; add turnips. Pour into a lightly greased 1-1/2-quart baking dish. Sprinkle breadcrumbs over top. Bake at 350 degrees F for 20 to 25 minutes, or until hot and bubbly.

Makes 6 servings

SIDE DISHES

Creamy Spinach Dip

- 1 (8-ounce) container sour cream
- 1 cup mayonnaise
- 1/2 teaspoon celery salt
- 1/2 teaspoon dill weed
- 1/4 cup chopped green onions
- 3 cups frozen cut leaf spinach, thawed and well drained
- 1 (8-ounce) can water chestnuts, drained and finely chopped
- 3 tablespoons chopped red bell pepper, if desired

• • • • • • • • • • • •

Combine all ingredients together in a bowl and mix well. Cover and refrigerate for at least 1 hour to blend flavors. Serve with fresh vegetables, chips or crackers.

Makes 8 to 10 servings

SIDE DISHES

Hot Spinach-Artichoke Dip

1 (10-ounce) package frozen chopped spinach
2 (13.75-ounce) cans artichoke hearts, drained
1/2 cup mayonnaise
1/2 cup sour cream
1 cup freshly grated Parmesan cheese
1 cup grated pepper jack cheese

• • • • • • • • • • • •

Heat the spinach in the microwave on high for 5 minutes; drain and squeeze out all water possible. Coarsely chop the artichoke hearts in a food processor. Combine all the ingredients except the pepper jack cheese in a large bowl and mix well. Pour into a lightly sprayed 2-quart casserole dish and sprinkle pepper jack cheese over top. Bake at 350 degrees F for 30 minutes.

Makes 8 to 10 servings

SIDE DISHES

Spinach

- 6 slices bacon, cooked crisp and crumbled, reserving 2 tablespoons drippings
- 2 tablespoons flour
- 5 to 6 green onions, finely chopped
- Seasoning salt to taste
- 1 to 2 (10-ounce) packages frozen spinach, cooked and drained

• • • • • • • • • • • •

Make sauce with reserved drippings, flour, onions and salt. Add spinach and cook until thickened, about 3 to 5 minutes. Sprinkle cooked bacon over top.

Makes 6 to 8 servings

> *Spinach is very important . . .*
> in our family. Dad went to join the army in Sallisaw, Oklahoma, at the courthouse in about 1943. My mother, brother and I sat on the lawn, along with many other families, waiting for my dad to come out and tell us when he would be leaving. Dad came out and said, "I am not going." Mother asked, "What is wrong with you?" Dad said, "Nothing, I am going to raise spinach for the army." That he did and started the rest of the story with our family working together to survive. Dad turned an obligation to his country into an asset for his family.

SIDE DISHES

Spinach and Cheese Casserole

- 1 cup flour
- 1 teaspoon salt
- 1 teaspoon baking powder
- 2 eggs, slightly beaten
- 1 cup milk
- 1/2 cup butter or margarine, melted
- 1 (10-ounce) package frozen chopped spinach, thawed and drained
- 1 (16-ounce) package grated sharp cheddar cheese

• • • • • • • • • • •

Combine flour, salt and baking powder. In a separate bowl, mix the eggs, milk and butter. Add the flour mixture and combine; then add spinach and cheese. Place in a greased 9 x 13-inch baking dish. Bake at 350 degrees F for about 30 minutes.

Makes 4 to 6 servings

SIDE DISHES

Spinach-Onion Dip

- 1 cup cottage cheese
- 1 tablespoon lemon juice
- 1 (10-ounce) package frozen spinach, thawed, drained and squeezed
- 1/2 cup sour cream
- 1/2 cup chopped fresh parsley
- 1/4 cup chopped green onions, both green and white parts
- 1/2 teaspoon hot pepper sauce

• • • • • • • • • • • •

Combine cottage cheese and lemon juice in a food processor and blend until smooth. Add spinach, sour cream, parsley, green onions and hot pepper sauce. Process until just mixed; cover and refrigerate at least 4 hours. Serve with chips or other dippers.

Makes 8 to 10 servings

> Dad paid local pickers ten cents for each 30-pound basket of spinach they picked. I got to hand out the dimes as they weighed in. I also made my debut as an entrepreneur when I made bologna sandwiches and sold them to the pickers for five cents each.

SIDE DISHES

Spinach Dip

1 (10-ounce) package frozen chopped spinach, thawed
1 (8-ounce) can water chestnuts, drained and chopped
1 (16-ounce) container sour cream
1/2 cup mayonnaise
1 envelope vegetable soup mix
1/2 teaspoon lemon juice

• • • • • • • • • • •

Drain the thawed spinach, and then place on a paper towel, squeezing out the liquid. Combine the spinach, water chestnuts and remaining ingredients; cover and chill for 1 hour. Serve with assorted fresh vegetables for dipping.

Makes 8 to 10 servings

Dad's Gardens . . .

Dad always made a garden large enough to feed an army. He had farmland in the bottom of Webbers Falls, Oklahoma, where he always made a garden along the edge of one of the fields. That garden was made for people to filch out of. (He had another garden at our house.)

One day he was driving around the fields and came across two ladies in the edge of his garden in the turnip greens. He stopped and ask them, "How are you ladies?" They answered, "Fine. Clifford Sloan told us we could get some of these greens." Dad said, "He did?" They said, "Yes, and you know he lives right over here in Webbers. Do you know where he lives?" My dad said, "Yes, I know where he lives, and if he told you to get some greens I will just help you." He helped them fill their two plastic garbage sacks full of greens, loaded them in their car and told them to enjoy their greens. Never told them he was Clifford Sloan. He loved that sort of thing.

Poultry

Let me tell ...

you how the recipes looked when I was young. This is what we had to do: clean, singe and cut a chicken into pieces for serving. Would you know what to do first? Well, first we would go out in the chicken yard and catch one. That sometimes took some doing. Then we would wring its neck or chop its head off with an ax at the wood pile. To pick off the feathers we had to dip the chicken in boiling water, and then singe it. When we finally got an oil-burning cook stove, we would light a burner and hold the picked chicken by the head and feet and pass it close to the fire to singe or burn off any feathers. Otherwise we had to build a fire in the wood cook stove, take the burner plate off so the flames could come up through it and hold and singe the chicken there. Sounds pretty gross, doesn't it? It was! Did you notice that I said hold it by the head? Yes, the head was still on if we wrung its neck; if not, we had to hold it by the neck. Then came the gutting. That's right, you heard me, gutting. We had to slit that chicken open down the middle and pull out all those things inside, called the guts. While doing that we would salvage the liver and gizzard. They didn't waste a thing in those days; too many to feed on too little. If they were boiling the chicken for dumplings or dressing they also cooked the feet.

POULTRY

Southern Fried Chicken

1 fryer chicken, cut up
2 to 3 cups buttermilk
2 to 3 cups shortening or oil
1 cup Bisquick
1 cup flour
Salt and pepper to taste

• • • • • • • • • • • •

Place chicken pieces in buttermilk, making sure it is all submerged; cover and refrigerate overnight if time permits. Otherwise leave in buttermilk as long as possible. Heat shortening or oil in frying pan, enough to cover chicken. While oil is heating, take chicken out of buttermilk one piece at a time, letting excess buttermilk drain off. Roll in Bisquick, flour, salt and pepper mixed together. When oil is hot, place chicken carefully in oil, one piece at a time. Reduce heat slightly and cook, turning occasionally, until tender and crispy. Drain on paper towels. May place chicken in baking dish covered with foil in a 325-degree F oven to keep warm and to make sure chicken is nice and done and tender.

Makes 4 to 6 servings

POULTRY

Sweet Spicy Chicken

- 1 (8-ounce) bottle Russian or Catalina salad dressing
- 2 envelopes dry onion soup mix
- 1 (8-ounce) jar apricot preserves
- 6 to 8 skinless chicken breast halves

• • • • • • • • • • • •

Lightly spray baking dish with cooking spray. Mix the dressing, onion soup mix and preserves together and let stand while chicken is cooking. Bake chicken uncovered, without turning, at 350 degrees F for 30 minutes; drain pan juices. Pour dressing mix over the drained chicken and bake another 20 to 30 minutes, or until hot and bubbly.

Makes 6 to 8 servings

POULTRY

Chicken and Dumplings

1 medium-size chicken, cut up
Water to cover in 8- to 10-quart saucepan
1 cup flour
1 cup Bisquick
1/4 teaspoon pepper
2 eggs
1/3 cup milk or more to make sticky dough

• • • • • • • • • • •

Cover chicken with water in the saucepan and cook until tender. (Cooking time will depend on the size of the chicken.) When chicken is tender, remove and reserve broth in saucepan. Set chicken aside.

While chicken is cooking, combine remaining ingredients and mix until a very stiff dough is formed. Roll out on a floured board to thickness desired. (I roll mine thin.) Cut into squares with a sharp knife and leave out on board. Sprinkle with additional flour and let set for at least 1 hour. (This is what toughens them, for softer dumplings, cook about 10 minutes after rolling them out).

When ready to cook dumplings, bring broth back to a rolling boil. Pick up a few dumplings and drop into boiling broth one at a time. Do not dust off excess flour; this will thicken the broth. Reduce heat, cover and cook about 5 minutes. Uncover and let simmer until tender. Debone chicken and lay on top of dumplings while simmering. If needed, thicken with 2 tablespoons cornstarch mixed with 1 tablespoon water.

MAKES 8 TO 10 SERVINGS

POULTRY

Chicken Potato Casserole

- 6 to 8 breaded chicken tenders
- 3 to 4 large potatoes, peeled and thinly sliced
- 1 (10-ounce) package frozen green peas
- 2 (10.75-ounce) cans cream of mushroom soup
- 3/4 soup can of water

• • • • • • • • • • • •

Brown chicken in a nonstick skillet. Layer potatoes in the bottom of a lightly sprayed casserole dish; add the peas for the second layer. Arrange chicken over peas in a single layer. Mix the soup with the water and blend with wire whisk until smooth. Pour over casserole. Bake at 350 degrees F for about 45 minutes to 1 hour, or until golden and potatoes are tender to fork test.

MAKES 6 TO 8 SERVINGS

> I actually call...
> this my funeral casserole. Why? Reason is it can be put together very fast and only takes about 1 hour to cook. You can have a full dinner, meat, potatoes, vegetables and gravy, to a friend or neighbor's house in no time when there is a death. That is what we do in the country; it expresses our love and concern.

POULTRY

White Chicken Chili

- 2-1/2 cups water
- 1 teaspoon lemon pepper
- 1 teaspoon cumin seed
- 4 boneless chicken breast halves
- 1 clove garlic, finely chopped
- 1 cup chopped onion
- 2 (8-ounce) cans white shoepeg corn, drained
- 2 (4-ounce) cans chopped green chiles, undrained
- 1 teaspoon ground cumin
- 2 to 3 tablespoons lime juice
- 2 (14-ounce) cans white or great Northern beans, undrained
- Tortilla chips
- Grated cheese

• • • • • • • • • • • •

Combine water with the lemon pepper and cumin seed; bring to a boil. Add the chicken and return to a boil. Reduce heat to a simmer and then cook 30 minutes, or until fork tender. Remove chicken from pan, reserving broth in same pan, and cut into small pieces; return to saucepan.

Spray a medium skillet with vegetable oil; cook garlic about 1 minute over low heat, careful not to burn. Add to the chicken. Saute onion in same skillet until tender. Add onion, corn, chiles, cumin and lime juice to the chicken mixture; bring to a boil. Add beans and simmer until thoroughly heated, about 45 minutes. Serve with tortilla chips and cheese on top.

Makes 6 to 8 servings

POULTRY

Oven Fried Chicken

Salt and pepper to taste
1 cut up fryer chicken

2 cups Bisquick
3/4 to 1 cup canola oil

• • • • • • • • • • • • •

Salt and pepper chicken, roll in Bisquick, making sure it is heavily coated, and place on a lightly sprayed baking sheet. I put a little extra Bisquick on top of each piece. I like the crispy breading. Drizzle the oil over top. Bake at 350 degrees F for about 25 to 30 minutes. Turn chicken over with spatula to get the breading on bottom and bake an additional 25 to 30 minutes, or until done in center.

Makes 6 to 8 servings

> *The Giblet Story*
> *The first year I was married to my first husband, we lived in a little tiny house in Tulsa. We were grown up and feeling tough. We invited his mother to come to Tulsa for Thanksgiving dinner. I did a pretty good job of making my first holiday meal. I did know how to cook; we had to learn in those days. I had cooked my first meal at age 6. We were getting ready to put the meal on the table and "Ma," her name to everyone, said, "Are you going to make any giblet gravy?" I said, "No, there wasn't any giblets." "Oh," she said. Wasn't that nice of her? When we were finished eating, we boned the turkey for future use. Guess what was in the center of the turkey in a paper bag?*

POULTRY

Pot Roasted Chicken

- 1 chicken, cut up, or about 9 to 10 breast halves
- 7 to 8 small new potatoes, scrubbed
- 4 to 5 whole small onions, peeled
- 4 medium carrots, peeled and cut into 3-inch pieces
- 1/2 cup dry white wine
- 1 (14-ounce) can chicken broth
- 1 tablespoon lemon juice
- 3 cloves garlic, chopped fine
- 1 teaspoon oregano
- 1/2 teaspoon thyme
- 1/4 teaspoon pepper
- 2 tablespoons chopped parsley

• • • • • • • • • • •

Arrange the chicken, potatoes, onions and carrots in a lightly sprayed baking dish. Mix wine, broth and lemon juice together. Pour over chicken and vegetables. Sprinkle garlic, oregano, thyme, pepper and parsley over top. Bake uncovered at 350 degrees F for 40 to 50 minutes, turning occasionally until chicken is fork tender.

Makes 8 to 10 servings

POULTRY

Turkey and Dressing

- 1 turkey-size cooking bag
- 2 tablespoons flour
- 1 (8- to 12-pound) turkey, thawed

Dressing
- 2 onions, chopped
- 1 stalk celery, chopped, about 2 cups
- 4 to 6 cups crumbled cornbread
- 2 to 4 tablespoons sage to taste
- Salt and pepper to taste
- 4 to 5 eggs, beaten
- 1 to 2 cups chicken broth
- 4 to 6 tablespoons butter

Giblet Gravy
- Turkey giblets
- 4 to 5 cups water
- 3 to 4 tablespoons shortening
- 4 to 5 tablespoons flour

• • • • • • • • • • •

Open turkey bag, add flour, shake to coat the inside and shake out excess flour.

To prepare turkey, trim all excess fat around neck and tail area, and reserve for giblet gravy. Place a wire rack in a roasting pan. Place the turkey in the bag, punch holes in the top of the bag to let steam escape. Place bagged turkey on rack and bake at 350 degrees F for 2-1/2 to 3 hours. Check cooking time on turkey; it depends on weight. Meat thermometer should read 180 degrees F when done.

POULTRY

Dressing

Combine onions and celery in a saucepan; cover with water and cook until crisp tender. Prepare the dressing to go into the oven in a separate baking dish. Do not stuff the turkey. Spray baking dish and make sure it will fit in the oven with turkey if you only have one oven. Add cooked onion and celery, along with some of the boiling water, to the cornbread. Add sage, salt, pepper, eggs and enough broth to make dressing medium thick, not runny. Pour into a baking dish. Cut butter into pieces and scatter over dressing. Bake 30 to 45 minutes, or until done and lightly browned on top.

Giblet Gravy

Place gizzard, heart and neck of turkey and reserved fat in a saucepan. Cover with water and cook until tender, about 1 to 2 hours. Add liver for last half hour. Remove neck and remaining giblets, reserving the broth. Cut giblets into small pieces and return to cooking broth.

In a skillet, melt shortening. When it is hot, stir in flour and continue stirring until browned. When browned, reduce heat, pour giblets and broth into gravy pan, a cup or so at a time, stirring with a wire whisk, to cook and remove any lumps until it reaches desired thickness. If not all the broth is needed, strain and add giblets to gravy.

Note: Giblet Gravy is usually a little thinner than regular country gravy.

Makes 8 to 10 servings

POULTRY

King Ranch Chicken

- 1/2 cup chopped onions
- 1/2 cup chopped green bell peppers
- 1 (10.75-ounce) can cream of mushroom soup
- 1 (10.75-ounce) can cream of chicken soup
- 1 can original Ro*Tel tomatoes
- 1 (9-ounce) bag Nacho Cheese Doritos
- 2 cups cooked and cubed chicken
- 2 cups grated cheddar cheese

• • • • • • • • • • •

Saute onions and bell peppers. Add soups and tomatoes; stir to blend then set aside. In a 9 x 13-inch baking dish, layer Doritos in bottom. Layer chicken over Doritos. Pour soup mixture over chicken. Sprinkle cheese over chicken. Bake at 350 degrees F for 30 minutes, or until hot and bubbly.

Makes 6 to 8 servings

Meats

My lifelong friend . . .
and I nicknamed each other when I was in the third grade and she was in fourth. Her nickname is "Rosita" and mine is "Penelope." Now where we got those I do not know, but that is what we have called each other for more than fifty years. We can be apart for years, call and pick up a conversation just like it was yesterday. We try to get together once a month now for lunch and laughs. She makes a room light up when she walks in, can sing, play the piano and is as neat as a pin. I don't know how she ever tolerated me. I love her dearly!

Her dad had an old Model T. He let us play in and with it. Can you imagine letting your kids play with your car? We would sit in it and pretend that we were going shopping or some such. Then he let us actually drive it forward a little ways and backward a little ways. What a thrill. And you thought your last adventure was exciting.

Her mother was a scream. She giggled, pranced, sang and laughed. Families were so much a family. No two or three cars, one running here the other running there. They went together.

See, you thought this was just going to be a recipe for meatloaf, didn't you? Instead you got a lesson in friends and family. I guess you could sort of call life a "meatloaf," don't you? Rosita gave me this recipe 50 years ago.

MEATS

Meatloaf

- 2/3 cup dry bread-crumbs
- 1/4 to 1/2 cup milk
- 1-1/2 pounds ground beef
- 2 eggs, slightly beaten
- 1/4 cup grated or finely chopped onion
- 1 teaspoon salt
- 1/2 teaspoon sage
- Dash of pepper

Sauce
- 3 tablespoons firmly packed brown sugar
- 1/4 cup ketchup
- 1/4 teaspoon nutmeg
- 1 teaspoon dry mustard

• • • • • • • • • • •

Soak breadcrumbs in milk; add remaining meatloaf ingredients and mix well. Shape into loaf or place into loaf pan and bake at 350 degrees F for about 45 minutes.

Sauce
Mix all sauce ingredients together, and then spread on meatloaf and bake an additional 10 to 15 minutes.

Makes 6 to 8 servings

Note: I double my sauce because I like it running down the sides of the meatloaf.

MEATS

Swiss Steak

1/4 cup shortening
Salt and pepper
2 pounds round steak, 3/4- to 1-inch thick, tenderized
1/2 to 3/4 cup flour
1 medium onion, sliced and separated into rings
1 small green bell pepper, sliced into rings or chopped
1 cup hot water
1 (15-ounce) can chopped tomatoes, with liquid

• • • • • • • • • • • •

Heat shortening in a skillet. Salt and pepper the meat, and then roll it in the flour. Brown on both sides in the hot pan. Transfer to a baking dish or cast-iron skillet or one that can go into the oven. Layer onion and bell peppers over meat. Add water to tomatoes and pour over top. Cover and bake at 350 degrees F for about 2 hours.

Makes 4 to 6 servings

MEATS

Sausage Potato Casserole

- 1 pound pork sausage
- 1 (10.75-ounce) can cream of mushroom soup
- 3/4 cup milk
- 1/2 cup chopped onion
- 1/2 teaspoon salt
- 1/4 teaspoon pepper
- 3 cups potatoes, sliced
- 1/4 cup butter
- 1 (8-ounce) bag grated cheddar cheese

• • • • • • • • • • •

Brown sausage and drain; set aside. Mix soup, milk, onion, salt and pepper together. In a large casserole dish layer potatoes, soup mixture and sausage; repeat layers again, ending with sausage. Dot with butter. Bake at 350 degrees F for 75 to 90 minutes. Sprinkle with cheese and return to oven until melted.

Makes 4 to 6 servings

MEATS

Pot Roast

2 tablespoons olive oil
1 (3- to 4-pound) beef or
   pork roast
1 clove garlic, peeled and
   thinly sliced
Flour
1 large onion, peeled and
   quartered

5 to 6 carrots, peeled and cut
   in half crossways
3 to 4 whole medium
   potatoes, peeled
1 (12-ounce) package brown
   gravy mix

• • • • • • • • • • • •

Heat oil in a Dutch oven. With knife, make slits in roast. Place a slice of garlic in slits at various places on both sides of roast. Flour roast, and then brown in roasting pan. Place onion, carrots and potatoes around the roast. Mix brown gravy according to package directions and pour over roast. Cover, bake at 350 degrees F for about 2-1/2 to 3 hours, or until tender, checking occasionally. Cooking time depends on size of roast.

Makes 4 to 6 servings

MEATS

Country-Fried Steaks

1/2 cup flour, divided
1/4 cup cornmeal
1/2 teaspoon salt
Pepper to taste
4 beef cube steaks, about 1 pound

1 egg
1 tablespoon milk
Oil, enough to cover bottom of skillet

Gravy
2 tablespoons butter
2 to 3 tablespoons flour
Salt and pepper to taste
1-1/2 to 1-3/4 cups milk

• • • • • • • • • • • •

Combine half of flour, cornmeal, salt and pepper; set aside. Flour steaks with remaining flour. Beat egg and milk; coat steaks in egg mixture, and then dredge in cornmeal mixture. Fry in oil over medium heat for 6 to 7 minutes on each side, or until browned and cooked as desired.

Gravy
After cooking the steaks, add butter to the drippings and stir in flour, salt and pepper. Stir until lightly browned and smooth. Gradually add milk, bring to a boil, cook and stir until it reaches desired thickness. Add a little water if too thick.

MAKES 4 SERVINGS

MEATS

Sausage Balls

1/2 cup water
2 cups Bisquick

1 pound spicy sausage
10 ounces grated cheddar cheese

• • • • • • • • • • • •

Mix water and Bisquick together to form dough. You may need to add a tiny touch more water. Stir in sausage and cheese; mix well, and then roll into balls. Bake at 350 degrees for 15 to 20 minutes, or until browned and sausage is done. May need to turn once.

Makes 8 servings

Metric Conversion Chart

Liquid and Dry Measures

U.S.	Canadian	Australian
¼ teaspoon	1 mL	1 ml
½ teaspoon	2 mL	2 ml
1 teaspoon	5 mL	5 ml
1 tablespoon	15 mL	20 ml
¼ cup	50 mL	60 ml
⅓ cup	75 mL	80 ml
½ cup	125 mL	125 ml
⅔ cup	150 mL	170 ml
¾ cup	175 mL	190 ml
1 cup	250 mL	250 ml
1 quart	1 liter	1 litre

Temperature Conversion Chart

Fahrenheit	Celsius
250	120
275	140
300	150
325	160
350	180
375	190
400	200
425	220
450	230
475	240
500	260

Index

A
Apple Pie, 31
Artichoke-Hot Spinach Dip, 105

B
Baked Turnips, 103
Banana: Bread, 60; Nut Cake, 11; Split Cake, 12
Basic Glaze, 26
Biscuits, 61; Soda, 67
Breads: 57–72; Banana, 60; Biscuits, 61; Cinnamon Rolls, 68; Corn Dodgers, 70; Corn Sticks, 71; Cornbread, 63; Curt's English Muffins, 72; Doughnuts, 68; English Muffin Casserole, 64; No Knead, 62; Old-Fashioned Oatmeal, 65; Refrigerator Rolls, 66; Soda Biscuits, 67; Sweet Roll Dough, 68; Yeast Rolls, 69
Breakfast, 73–82; Casserole, 79; Chocolate Gravy, 78; French Toast, 81; Ham and Cheese Breakfast Casserole, 74; Muffins, 75; Oatmeal Pancakes, 80; Omelet, 77; Pancake or Waffle Batter, 76
Breakfast Casserole, 79
Broccoli Casserole, 98
Brown Sugar Frosting, 24
Brownie Sheet Cake, 13

C
Cabbage, Quick Fix, 99
Cakes, 7–23; Banana Nut, 11; Banana Split, 12; Brownie Sheet, 13; Carrot, 10; Crushed Pineapple, 14; Fruit Cocktail, 15; Johnny Cake, 16; Lemon Gelatin, 18; Mississippi Mud, 19; Nola's Pineapple, 22; Oatmeal, 20; One Egg, 17; Pumpkin, 21; Strawberry, 23
Candied Sweet Potatoes, 102
Caramel Corn, 55
Carrots: Candied, 102; Cake, 10
Casserole: Breakfast, 79; Broccoli, 98; Chicken Potato, 116; Corn and Rice, 97; English Muffin, Bread, 64; Ham and Cheese Breakfast, 74; Sausage Potato, 127; Spinach and Cheese, 107
Chicken: and Dumplings, 115; King Ranch, 122; Oven-Fried, 118; Pot Roasted, 119; Potato Casserole, 116; Salad, 89; Southern Fried, 113; Sweet Spicy, 114; White Chili, 117.
Chili, White Chicken, 117
Chocolate: Cocoa Frosting, 24; Gravy, 78; Pie, 30
Chocolate Gravy, 78
Chocolate Pie, 30
Chunky Potato Salad, 91
Cinnamon Rolls, 68
Cobbler, Hot Fruit, 43
Cocoa Frosting, 24
Coconut Custard Pie, 32
Cookies: 45–55; Corn Flake, 54; Crisp

Sugar Drop, 50;
Date Bars, 49;
Kookie Brittle, 48;
Oatmeal Drop, 51;
Potato Chip, 52; Soft
Molasses, 53
Corn: Caramel, 55;
Corn and Rice
Casserole, 97; Corn
Flake Cookies, 54;
Cornbread, 63;
Cornbread Salad,
86; Dodgers, 70;
Johnny Cake, 16;
Shoepeg Corn
Salad, 85; Sticks, 71
Corn Dodgers, 70
Corn Flake Cookies,
54
Corn Sticks, 71
Cornbread, 63
Country-Fried Steaks,
129
Creamy Spinach Dip,
104
Crisp Sugar Drop
Cookies, 50
Crushed Pineapple
Cake, 14
Crusts: 35; Crumb, 43;
Flaky, 44; Pie, 44
Curt's English Muffins,
72
Custard: Coconut Pie,
32; Ruby's Pie, 33

D

Date Bars, 49
Dips: Creamy Spinach,
104; Hot Spinach-
Artichoke, 105;
Spinach-Onion, 108
Doughnuts, 68

E

English Muffin:
Casserole Bread, 64;
Curt's, 72
English Muffin
Casserole Bread, 64

F

Five-Layer Pie, 34
French Toast: 81;
Overnight, 82
Fresh Strawberry Pie,
37
Frostings: 13-15, 18-
20, 23; Basic Glaze,
26; Brown Sugar, 24;
Brown Sugar Sea
Foam, 25; Caramel,
25; Cocoa, 24;
Chocolate, 25;
Harvest Moon, 26;
Seven-Minute, 25
Frozen Fluffy
Strawberry Pie, 36
Fruit Cocktail Cake, 15

G

Gelatin: Lemon Cake,
18; Strawberry
Salad, 90

H

Ham and Cheese
Breakfast Casserole,
74
Harvest Moon
Frosting, 26
Hot Fruit Cobbler, 43
Hot Spinach-
Artichoke Dip, 105

I

Icings, see Frostings

J

Johnny Cake, 16

K

King Ranch Chicken,
122
Kookie Brittle, 48

L

Layered Salad, 93
Lemon Gelatin Cake,
18

M

Macaroni Salad, 87
Meatloaf, 125
Meats: 123-129;
Country-Fried
Steaks, 129;
Meatloaf, 125; Pot
Roast, 128; Sausage

Roast, 128; Sausage Balls, 130; Sausage Potato Casserole, 127; Swiss Steak, 126
Meringue, 30
Millionaire Pie, 35
Mississippi Mud Cake, 19
Mock Apple Pie, 42
Mock Pecan Pie, 39
Molasses, Soft Cookies, 53
Muffins, 75

N

Nola's Pineapple Cake, 22

O

Oatmeal: Cake, 20; Drop Cookies, 51; Old-Fashioned Oatmeal Bread, 65; Pancakes, 80
Oatmeal Cake, 20
Oatmeal Drop Cookies, 51
Oatmeal Pancakes, 80
Old-Fashioned Oatmeal Bread, 65
Omelet, 77
One-Cup Salad, 92
Onion-Spinach Dip, 108
Oven-Fried Chicken, 118
Overnight French Toast, 82

P

Pancakes: 76; Oatmeal, 80
Pancake or Waffle Batter, 76
Pecan Pie, 40
Pies, 27-44; Apple, 31; Chocolate, 30; Coconut Custard, 32; Five-Layer, 34; Fresh Strawberry, 37; Frozen Fluffy Strawberry, 36; Hot Fruit Cobbler, 43; Mock Apple, 42; Mock Pecan, 39; Millionaire, 35; Pecan, 40; Tomato, 100; Ruby's Custard, 33; Squash, 38; Pumpkin, 41
Pineapple: Crushed, Cake, 14; Nola's, Cake, 22; Scalloped, 101
Pink Stuff, 94
Pot Roast, 129
Pot Roasted Chicken, 119
Potato: Chunky, Salad, 91; Chip Cookies, 52; Salad, 88; Candied Sweet, 102; Chicken, Casserole, 116; Sausage, Casserole, 127; Potato Chip Cookies, 52
Potato Salad, 88
Poultry, 111-122; Chicken and Dumplings, 115; Chicken Potato Casserole, 116; Chicken Salad, 89; King Ranch Chicken, 122; Oven-Fried Chicken, 118; Pot Roasted Chicken, 119; Southern Fried Chicken, 113; Sweet Spicy Chicken, 114; Turkey and Dressing, 120; White Chicken Chili, 117
Pumpkin: Cake, 21; Pie, 41
Pumpkin Cake, 21
Pumpkin Pie, 41

Q

Quick Fix Cabbage, 99

R

Refrigerator Rolls, 66
Rolls: Cinnamon, 68; Refrigerator, 66;

Sweet Roll Dough, 68; Yeast, 69
Ruby's Custard Pie, 33

S
Salads: 83–94; Chicken, 89; Chunky Potato, 91; Cornbread, 86; Layered, 93; Macaroni, 87; One-Cup, 92; Pink Stuff, 94; Potato, 88; Shoepeg Corn, 85; Strawberry Gelatin, 90
Sausage Balls, 130
Sausage Potato Casserole, 127
Scalloped Pineapple, 101
Seven-Minute Frosting, 25
Shoepeg Corn Salad, 85
Side Dishes: 95–110; Baked Turnips, 103; Broccoli Casserole, 98; Candied Sweet Potatoes, 102; Corn and Rice Casserole, 97; Creamy Spinach Dip, 104; Hot Spinach-Artichoke Dip, 105; Quick Fix Cabbage, 99; Scalloped Pineapple, 101; Spinach and Cheese Casserole, 107; Spinach, 106; Spinach Dip, 109; Spinach-Onion Dip, 108; Tomato Pie, 100
Soda Biscuits, 67
Soft Molasses Cookies, 53
Southern Fried Chicken, 113
Spinach: 104–109; and Cheese Casserole, 107; Creamy, Dip, 104; Dip, 109; Hot-Artichoke Dip, 105; -Onion Dip, 108; Spinach, 106
Squash Pie, 38
Strawberry: Cake, 23; Frozen Fluffy, Pie, 36; Fresh, Pie, 37; Gelatin Salad, 90
Strawberry Cake, 23
Strawberry Gelatin Salad, 90
Sweet Roll Dough, 68
Sweet Potatoes, Candied, 102
Sweet Spicy Chicken, 114
Swiss Steak, 126

T
Tomato Pie, 100
Turkey and Dressing, 120
Turnips, Baked, 103

W
Waffle and Pancake Batter, 76
White Chicken Chili, 117

Y
Yeast Rolls, 69